MW00649115

Kohelet: A Map to Eden
An Intertextual Journey

David Curwin

KOHELET
A Map to Eden
· · · · · · ·
AN INTERTEXTUAL JOURNEY

Aleph Beta Press
Maggid Books

Kohelet: A Map to Eden
An Intertextual Journey
First Edition, 2023

Maggid Books
An imprint of Koren Publishers Jerusalem Ltd.

POB 8531, New Milford, CT 06776-8531, USA
& POB 4044, Jerusalem 9104001, Israel
www.korenpub.com

Aleph Beta Press
info@alephbeta.org
www.alephbeta.org

The publication of this book was made possible
through the generous support of *The Jewish Book Trust.*

ISBN 978-1-59264-611-1, *hardcover*

Printed and bound in the United States

*In honor of Rabbi Fohrman
and the Aleph Beta team*

*Whose love for God and passion for the Torah
kindles the hearts of the faithful
and renews all of God's people in the fire of His love.*

וְהָלְכוּ גּוֹיִם רַבִּים וְאָמְרוּ לְכוּ
וְנַעֲלֶה אֶל־הַר־ה׳ וְאֶל־בֵּית אֱלֹהֵי יַעֲקֹב
וְיוֹרֵנוּ מִדְּרָכָיו וְנֵלְכָה בְּאֹרְחֹתָיו
כִּי מִצִּיּוֹן תֵּצֵא תוֹרָה וּדְבַר־ה׳ מִירוּשָׁלָם׃

(Micah 4:2)

Author's Dedication

This book is dedicated to the loving memory of my father

Dr. Richard Curwin
(1944–2018)

We didn't get to celebrate its publication together,
but your decades of support and wisdom
motivated me to take on the project and inspired me to finish.

Contents

Introduction

Ever since I was young, I loved following along with the yearly reading cycle of books of the Tanakh. However, the book of *Kohelet* (Ecclesiastes) was probably the least compelling. Longer than any other book ritually read, and with no story to follow, many repetitive phrases and a generally gloomy atmosphere, I typically tuned out when it was chanted on the festival of Sukkot.

However, I recently discovered the treasure of intertextual study, primarily through the teachings of Rabbi David Fohrman and his staff at Aleph Beta, a website and resource center for Jewish learning. In this method, two distinct biblical texts are compared, and the language and themes common to both help shed light on each. After another Sukkot – and another reading of Kohelet where I felt disconnected from the text – I came home and told myself there must be something more to be found here. Perhaps the book is connected to another biblical text. While rereading Kohelet, without the aid of a computerized search tool, or even a concordance, I sensed a strong connection to the first chapters of Bereshit. The more I looked, the more I found.

This work is the fruit of that study. It took me all over the Tanakh, to places I never expected to reach. I hope you, the reader, will enjoy the journey as much as I have.

A couple of notes to help you along the way:

Intertextual study requires a sensitivity to the original Hebrew text. As is obvious by now, I have authored this book in English, despite the challenges involved. While most of the translated verses are based on *The Koren Tanakh – Magerman Edition*, I have frequently modified the translation, occasionally borrowing phrases from other published translations (see Bibliography). To better reflect the Hebrew allusions necessary to understand the connections between different texts, I have often chosen a translation that emphasizes literalness over clarity.

Although anglicized terms for books and names might be more familiar to some readers, due to the focus on linguistic messages found in the words of the text, I have used transliterations from the original Hebrew. For example, the words *Kohelet* and *Hevel* reflect the intent of the biblical text much more than do Ecclesiastes and Abel. For the convenience of those not familiar with the transliterated Hebrew terms used, I have provided a glossary at the end of the book.

Acknowledgments

Every book is the culmination of the author's education, experiences, and interactions with others. No work of writing is born in a vacuum. And yet, I feel that for this book, I am even more in need to acknowledge those who helped bring it to fruition. When the ideas presented here first came to me, I wasn't sure what to do with them. A class? An essay? Having never written a book, that seemed like a remote possibility. But with the help of those mentioned below, that dream became a reality.

First and foremost on this list is, without question, Rabbi David Fohrman, founder and lead scholar of Aleph Beta. I first encountered Rabbi Fohrman through his recorded classes and books. Later, I was privileged to attend his lectures in person. From his presentations, I developed an appreciation for biblical intertextuality (which formed the basis of this work). That in itself would have been sufficient to give thanks here. But I was so very fortunate to develop a personal relationship with him as well. This led to one of my first opportunities to present my theories about Kohelet, where Rabbi Fohrman gave me incredibly helpful feedback and connected me with other scholars who provided additional insights. And yet, that still wasn't enough. He encouraged me to turn my thoughts into a book, and then made sure it happened by connecting me with the wonderful people at Koren Publishers, and working with them to see that the book would indeed be published. I really can't thank you enough. My wish for you, which would be a blessing for me and all lovers of Torah, is that you continue to "make many books" (Kohelet 12:12).

In addition to the scholars of Aleph Beta that Rabbi Fohrman introduced me to, I also presented my early ideas on Kohelet to the Friday night *ḥabura* on Pitum Haketoret in Efrat, led faithfully for years by Micah Gimpel. Participants in this *ḥabura* (myself included) don't go easy on any speaker, challenging their thesis from every direction. I knew that if my unconventional ideas about Kohelet passed their test of fire, I'd be in good shape with any future audience. I look forward to learning with all of them for many years to come.

Transforming the ideas in my head into a detailed book required inestimable hours of research, writing, and editing. By my nature, I constantly reach out to people, whether they know me or not, for advice and answers. I was fortunate to have such terrific people reading my requests, without whom no one would be reading this right now. For all their time and effort, I'd like to thank David Bar-Cohn, Avi Baumol, Yoel Bin-Nun, Erica Brown, Yuval Cherlow, Rafi Eis, Karyn Goldberger, Jonathan Grossman, Zvi Grumet, Malka Hubscher, Yoel Kortick, Seth Kosowsky, Steve Kowarsky, Nathan Laufer, Alex Maged, Simi Peters, Elhanan Samet, Ami Silver, Ezra Zuckerman Sivan, Avraham Stav, Rivky Stern, Yael Unterman, Elisheva Urbas, Barry Waldman, and Jonathan Wiesen. A special thanks goes to my friend and mentor, Jeffrey Saks, who always made sure I was heading in the right direction.

The document was first edited by Deena Nataf and fact-checked by David Mishkin. They transformed the writings of an enthusiastic layman into a professional manuscript. Reading the book after they worked on it gave me the confidence that it should be published and shared with the world.

And when it finally came to publishing, Koren was my highest aspiration. I've been a huge fan ever since I first acquired their Tanakh and siddur decades ago. We Hebraicized our name to "Koren" in Hebrew when moving to Israel – while the primary factor was its similarity to Curwin, the prestige of Koren surely inspired me as well. Watching Koren, and its imprint Maggid Books, become the premier publishers of Torah content over the past few years has been incredibly satisfying, and having my book published by them was everything I could have asked for. Thank you so much to Matthew Miller, Reuven Ziegler, Caryn Meltz, Ita Olesker, Tani Bayer, Aryeh Grossman, Rachelle Emanuel, and Dvora Rhein for your fulfillment of my dream and your contributions to the Jewish people.

As I get to the end of these acknowledgments, I am drawn to the more personal. My interest in studying Torah began in the Hebrew Academy of San Francisco and blossomed in my years of study at Yeshivat HaKibbutz HaDati in Ein Tzurim. While sadly neither of those institutions remains open today, their legacy will remain for generations. In particular, I must thank the teachers who opened the doors of studying Torah to me: Mordechai Rindenow, Mitch Heifetz, and Shimon Heksher *z"l*, David Bigman and Avia Hacohen. Likewise, without my eternal *ḥavruta*, Raffi Lev-Tzion, I couldn't have ever considered a project like this.

My family was a source of great support throughout the years of this endeavor. Both my mother, Geri Curwin, and my in-laws, Rob and Sue Kaplan, always provided encouragement and assistance whenever I needed it. A special thanks must go to my brother and sister-in-law, Aaron and Sarete Kaplan, who for years have hosted us in their home for Shabbat Ḥol HaMoed Sukkot, when Kohelet is read. It was in their home, in 2017, when I first became

Acknowledgments

determined to investigate the message behind Kohelet. And again the following year, when I related my discoveries in their sukka, Aaron asked me a question I hadn't considered, "Why is Kohelet read on Sukkot?" which became an appendix to this book. I look forward to sharing this book in your sukka in the years to come.

Lastly, I must thank my children: Yocheved and Zev Baker, Betzalel Curwin, and Noa Curwin. I know that my obsession with Kohelet must have seemed a bit much to you, but you never stopped encouraging me, and pushing me forward. The book of Kohelet is occupied with the question of legacy, and I couldn't ask for a better legacy than the one I know you do and will provide.

And of course, just like everything else in my life, I couldn't have taken a single step in this project without my hand being held by my darling wife, Toby. You gave me the time for this, you ignored my concerns of imposter syndrome and insisted that I march forth, you gave me happy emojis for every piece of news about the book, and of course you were always willing to read anything I wanted your insightful eyes to inspect. Even if I don't show it as I should, you are a ceaseless inspiration to me. Kohelet put it best: "Enjoy life with the woman you love" (Kohelet 9:9). I am blessed that you are that woman.

Kohelet and Shlomo

Chapter 1

The Kohelet Narrative

Of the five *megillot* in the Tanakh, three describe historical events (Rut, Eikha and Esther) and one uses a narrative format to express poetic themes (Shir HaShirim). Only one, Kohelet, appears as an outlier, with no story being told. Rather, its author reflects on his life experiences, passing lessons on to the reader. In this regard, it is classified as wisdom literature, and can be compared to other biblical books of that genre such as Mishlei. But unlike Mishlei, Kohelet remains one of the *megillot*, all of which tell a story.

After a closer examination of Kohelet, I discovered that its lessons do indicate a story. The prose comprising the four main themes of the book – much of what we do in life is futile, searching for knowledge does not lead to a positive end, death is inevitable, and the righteous suffer while the wicked prosper – contains one recurring word: *hevel*.

Kohelet's themes and one-word motif seem to have been inspired by a much earlier story: that of Adam, the first man. Adam's story is the inspiration for this project.

In this book, we will examine the parallels between the lives of Shlomo and Adam. We will also see strong textual connections between those opening chapters of Bereshit that are germane to Adam and the verses in Kohelet. But our journey will not end there. A third story, the episode of the spies in the book of Bemidbar, also has thematic and literary parallels to the stories of Adam and Shlomo. Moreover, each narrative is immediately followed by stories of rebellion and disputes over the way to sacrifice to God: Kayin and Hevel, Koraḥ, and Yorovam.

By comparing all three stories, a picture will begin to emerge of what led to the downfalls and subsequent rebellions described in each episode, and how they can be avoided in the future. The answers can be found in the laws of the Torah, which was given to help put us on the correct path. We will show how laws as disparate as tzitzit, the Yom Kippur service, and the *hak'hel* ceremony[1] play a role in preventing the pitfalls we will see repeated again and again. At times we will depart from the text of Kohelet for other biblical texts. But the messages of Kohelet – what leads to downfalls, how to avoid them, and how to return to a successful path – will remain the focus of this book throughout.

We will begin our exploration with Shlomo, the author of Kohelet.

---

1. A national assembly held every seven years, where the king reads from the Torah to the people. For more on *hak'hel*, see ch. 23.

WHO WAS KOHELET?

Kohelet[2] is traditionally ascribed to Shlomo son of David – the second king in the Davidic dynasty.[3] An opinion in the Midrash[4] claims that Shlomo wrote Shir HaShirim in his youth, Mishlei in middle age, and Kohelet at the end of his life.

Shlomo's name does not appear in Kohelet, but there are solid reasons to accept his identification with the narrator. First, the text opens with the statement, "The sayings of Kohelet son of David, king in Jerusalem" (Kohelet 1:1). Several verses later, the narrative continues, "I, Kohelet, was king of Israel in Jerusalem" (1:12). Shlomo was David's son who was king in Jerusalem. He was also the only descendant of David to rule over all of Israel, for after his death the kingdom split in two, and the Davidic dynasty ruled only the southern kingdom of Yehuda.[5]

---

2. Kohelet is both the name of the book and the author's pseudonym. It appears to derive from the Hebrew root K-H-L, "to gather" or "to assemble." Many theories have been proposed as to why the name Kohelet was chosen. We will present our theory in chapter 23.

3. For the purposes of this work, I am not going to tackle the question of when the book of Kohelet was composed. Even the Sages, who universally agree that Shlomo was the author of Kohelet (along with Shir HaShirim and Mishlei, where Shlomo's name appears explicitly), write in Bava Batra 15a that generations later, "[King] Hizkiya and his colleagues composed" those books. (And even later, according to *Avot DeRabbi Natan* 1:4, the Men of the Great Assembly returned Kohelet to the biblical canon after properly explaining it.) Bin-Nun and Medan quote Prof. Moshe Ben Asher and Prof. Yehezkel Kaufmann as saying the late "sealing" of Kohelet can explain the frequent use of post-biblical Hebrew and the influence of Aramaic and Persian on the language of the book (Yoel Bin-Nun and Yaakov Medan, *Ani Kohelet* [Jerusalem: Maggid Books, 2017], 66). However, as we will continue to demonstrate, whoever edited the final work firmly linked the themes in Kohelet with the life of Shlomo. I follow the approach put forward by Micha Goodman, who writes that his method of interpretation is literary and synchronic, and he reads the way a book asks to be read. Kohelet asks to be read as the reflections of Shlomo (Micha Goodman, *HaNe'um HaAharon shel Moshe* [Or Yehuda: Kinneret, Zmora-Bitan, Dvir, 2014], 272).

4. *Shir HaShirim Rabba* 1:10.

5. Michael V. Fox, *The JPS Bible Commentary: Ecclesiastes* (Philadelphia: The Jewish Publication Society, 2004), pp. ix–x.

While it is possible to claim that the above verses refer only to a descendant of David and not to Shlomo himself,[6] the content of Kohelet portrays a king whose life matches only that of Shlomo. Kohelet describes a wise king, who built extensively. It recounts his wealth and his many wives. No king fits this better than Shlomo.

A BIOGRAPHY OF SHLOMO

A review of Shlomo's life will enable us to better understand the connection between Shlomo and Kohelet, particularly his relationship with God. Moreover, it will be invaluable for our exploration of both the book of Kohelet itself and the parallels to the other stories we will be examining further on.

Shlomo first appears in the book of Shmuel. He is the child of King David and Batsheva. From his very birth, he had a special relationship with God, even meriting having a special name bestowed on him by the Almighty: "The Lord loved him, and He sent a message through the prophet Natan, naming him Yedidya ("the Lord's beloved")" (Shmuel II 12:24–25).

He next appears many chapters later, in the first book of Melakhim. In chapter 1, we read of the struggle over who would succeed David as king. Shlomo's right to the throne was challenged

---

6. One argument against Shlomo's being the king referred to in Kohelet is 1:16, where Kohelet says he surpassed "anyone who has ruled over Jerusalem before" him, עַל כָּל־אֲשֶׁר־הָיָה לְפָנַי עַל־יְרוּשָׁלָָ. This would seem to indicate a king much later in the dynasty. However, the same phrasing is found in a description of Shlomo himself:

וַיְגַדֵּל יְהוָה אֶת־שְׁלֹמֹה לְמַעְלָה לְעֵינֵי כָּל־יִשְׂרָאֵל וַיִּתֵּן עָלָיו הוֹד מַלְכוּת אֲשֶׁר לֹא־
הָיָה עַל־כָּל־מֶלֶךְ לְפָנָיו עַל־יִשְׂרָאֵל:

The Lord granted Shlomo supreme greatness in the eyes of all Israel and endowed him with a royal majesty beyond that of any king of Israel **before him**. (Divrei HaYamim I 29:25)

Just as the verse in Divrei HaYamim praises Shlomo over his predecessors, so too does the verse in Kohelet.

by his brother Adoniya, but in the end Shlomo was accepted as king by all.

In the following chapter, we read of David's deathbed instructions to Shlomo. He begins with this charge:

> I am going the way of all the earth; you must be strong and prove yourself a man. You must keep the charge of the Lord your God, following His ways and keeping His laws and commandments, His rulings and decrees, as written in the teaching of Moshe. For then you will succeed in whatever you do, wherever you turn. For then, the Lord will fulfill the promise He made to me, saying: "If your sons keep to their path and walk before Me truly, with all their heart and all their soul, then no one of your lineage will be cut off from the throne of Israel." (Melakhim I 2:2–4)

This mission would follow Shlomo for the rest of his life – for good and for bad.

Chapter 3 of Melakhim I begins with praise of Shlomo mixed with implied criticism that he did not fully follow in the ways of his father:

> Shlomo formed a marriage alliance with King Pharaoh of Egypt; he took Pharaoh's daughter in marriage and brought her to the City of David until he had finished building his palace, the House of the Lord, and the wall around Jerusalem. But the people were sacrificing at the high shrines, for at that time a House for the Lord's name had not yet been built. Shlomo loved the Lord and followed the laws of his father David, but he still offered sacrifices and incense at the high shrines. (3:1–3)

SHLOMO RECEIVES THE GIFT OF WISDOM

Despite deviating to some degree from the ways of his father, his relationship with God remained intact, as evidenced by his famous dream where he asked for, and received, the gift of wisdom:

> At Givon, the Lord appeared to Shlomo in a dream. And God said, "Ask – what shall I give you?" And Shlomo said, "You treated Your servant David, my father, with great kindness, for he walked before You in truth and in justice, and with a sincere heart toward You. And You have maintained this great kindness for him by granting him a son and heir to his throne, as is now the case. And now, O Lord, my God, You made Your servant king in my father David's place, but I am a young boy; I have no experience as a leader…. Grant Your servant an understanding heart to judge Your people, to distinguish between good and bad, for who can judge this immense people of Yours?"
>
> And it pleased the Lord that Shlomo had made this request, and God said to him, "Because this is the request you made – you did not ask for long life, or for wealth, or for the lives of your enemies, but you asked for wisdom to discern in judgment – I have fulfilled your words. Here, I am granting you a wise, discerning heart – no one like you has ever been before you, and no one like you will ever rise again after you. But what is more, I am granting you what you did not ask for, both wealth and honor – not a man among kings will compare to you for as long as you live. And if you follow in My ways and keep My laws and commandments, as your father David did, then I shall grant you long life." (Melakhim I 3:5–14)

Like Adam and Ḥava in the Garden of Eden, Shlomo also sought the knowledge "to distinguish between good and bad [*ra*]."[7] Their pursuit of that knowledge ended in disaster (which we will examine in depth in section two, chapter 11). Why, then, was God pleased with Shlomo's request? The reason is that Shlomo wanted that knowledge in order to *serve* God, whereas Adam and Ḥava desired it in order to be *like* God (Bereshit 3:5, 22).[8] They took the fruit of knowledge without permission, whereas Shlomo, recognizing that God is the source of knowledge, asked God for it. While in some respects this seemed like a repeat of the Garden story, it got off to a much more auspicious start.

God granted Shlomo wisdom and added what Shlomo did not request: wealth and glory. However, it is important to note that God's last promise, regarding the length of Shlomo's reign,[9] was contingent on Shlomo's following the "laws and commandments, as [his] father David did."[10]

Immediately following the dream comes the story of the two women both claiming to be the mother of a baby, whom the king famously suggested splitting in two. In response, the people recognized his wisdom. But they did not merely comprehend that he was wise. They saw that his wisdom came from God, and was

---

7. The Hebrew word *ra* can mean both "evil" and "bad." Throughout this book, I will translate it according to the context, even though neither translation fully captures the nuance of *ra*.

8. Avi Ehrlich, *Ancient Zionism: The Biblical Origins of the National Idea* (New York: The Free Press, 1995), 148.

9. Bin-Nun and Medan (*Ani Kohelet*, 127–128) maintain that the length of days in the prophecy refers not to Shlomo's lifespan but to the endurance of his dynasty, as is mentioned explicitly in the Torah in its enumeration of the laws of kings: "He and his descendants will reign long in the midst of Israel" (Devarim 17:20). Since Shlomo did not follow the laws, he did not merit descendants who would have reigns as successful as his.

10. Rashi and Radak on Melakhim I 3:14.

7

intended to assist him in his execution of justice: "When all of Israel heard about the case that the king had judged, they feared the king, for they saw that the wisdom of God was within him to do justice" (Melakhim I 3:28).

As we continue to read of the success of Shlomo's reign, his wisdom is frequently recalled, but always with the added comment that God granted it to him:

> God had granted wisdom to Shlomo, and deep understanding, and a mind as broad as the sand upon the seashore. Shlomo's wisdom surpassed the wisdom of all the peoples of the East and all the wisdom of Egypt. He was wiser than any other man.... He composed three thousand proverbs, and his songs numbered a thousand and five. And he spoke of the trees, from the cedar in Lebanon to the hyssop that grows out of walls; and he spoke of the beasts and the birds and the creeping creatures and the fish. People from all nations came to hear Shlomo's wisdom on behalf of all the kings of the earth who had heard of his wisdom. (Melakhim I 5:9–14)
> The Lord had endowed Shlomo with wisdom, as He had promised him. (5:26)

SHLOMO'S KINGDOM BEGINS TO RESEMBLE EGYPT

The following chapters in Melakhim discuss the building and consecration of the Temple in Jerusalem. As noted in Melakhim I 6:1, this project was the culmination of the process that began 480 years before, when Israel first left Egypt. As such, it should be viewed as the pinnacle of the relationship between God and Israel, with Shlomo finally providing God with a permanent home. The extensive description of the building of the Temple and all its vessels demonstrates the significance of this event.

However, mixed in with these verses are some statements that provide a different context to the state of Shlomo's reign. For example, in the middle of a section discussing the panels of the House (the Temple) and a description of the walls of the House, we find the following:

> And the word of the Lord came to Shlomo: "Concerning this House that you are building: If you follow My laws and uphold My rulings and keep all My commandments by following them, then I will fulfill My promise through you, the promise that I made to your father David. I will dwell in the midst of the Israelites, and I will never abandon My people Israel." (Melakhim I 6:11–13)

While God's promise demonstrates His commitment to Israel, the conditional nature of the prophecy indicates that Shlomo needed to be reminded of his obligations while involved in this massive project.

Although at this point there are no signs of Shlomo's abandoning God's laws, rules, and commandments, the verses hint to dark parallels with a more sinister building project. A brief glimpse of this can be found earlier, at the beginning of the narrative describing the building: "King Shlomo began to levy forced labor upon all of Israel; the levy was thirty thousand men" (Melakhim I 5:27). The Hebrew word for "forced labor" and "levy" here is *mas*. It is the same word used to describe the forced labor imposed by Pharaoh on Israel in Egypt: "So they placed slave masters over the Israelites to oppress them with forced labor [*mas*]; they built supply towns [*arei miskenot*] for Pharaoh: Pitom and Ramesses" (Shemot 1:11). But the comparison does not end there; it appears in the book of Melakhim again, more explicitly, a few chapters after the one cited above:

> For these purposes, King Shlomo imposed forced labor [*mas*]: to build the House of the Lord and his own house,

the Milo, the wall of Jerusalem, Ḥatzor, Megiddo, and Gezer. Pharaoh, king of Egypt, had marched up and captured Gezer – he burned it with fire and killed the Canaanite inhabitants of the city – and he gave it as a wedding gift to his daughter, Shlomo's wife. Shlomo built Gezer, lower Beit Ḥoron, Baalat, and Tadmor in the wilderness in the region, as well as all of Shlomo's supply towns [*arei miskenot*], chariot towns, and cavalry towns – all that Shlomo desired to build in Jerusalem, Lebanon, and throughout the land of his dominion. (Melakhim I 9:15–19)

Not only do we again see the forced labor (*mas*), but there is also mention of supply towns – *arei miskenot* – the same type that Israel was forced to build for Pharaoh in Egypt.

While three verses later the text does qualify the situation slightly by distinguishing between "forced labor" and "slavery": "Shlomo never reduced the Israelites to slavery" (Melakhim I 9:22), the linguistic parallels to the Egyptian slavery (along with the actual political alliance with Egypt) cannot be ignored.

We saw how on the one hand there was major progress in the journey from Egypt to Jerusalem, yet on the other hand we see that Israel is once again facing many of the same forms of oppression from which they suffered in Egypt centuries before.

Shlomo's long speech at the dedication of the Temple appears in Melakhim I, chapter 8. It mentions Egypt multiple times, all in the positive context of recalling God's redemption of Israel:

"Blessed is the Lord, God of Israel," he said, "who made a promise to my father David with His own mouth and has now fulfilled it with His own hand, saying: 'From the day I brought My people, Israel, out of Egypt, I never chose a city from among all the tribes of Israel, to build a House

where My name would be; but I chose David to be over
My people Israel.'" (Melakhim I 8:15–16)
    And there I have set a place for the Ark, which contains
the covenant that the Lord made with our ancestors when
He brought them out of the land of Egypt. (8:21)
    For they are Your people and Your share, whom You
brought out from Egypt, from the midst of the iron crucible.
Let Your eyes be open to the plea of Your servant and the
plea of Your people Israel; listen to them whenever they call
out to You. For You set them apart from all the other peoples
of the land as Your own share, as You promised through
Moshe, Your servant, when You brought our ancestors out
of Egypt, O Lord God. (8:51–53)

At this point in the story, the references to Egypt appear to be
positive. In fact, it could be understood that this was the culmination of the process that began with the exodus from Egypt centuries before: Israel was fully liberated from all of its enemies, and
even Pharaoh was subservient to Israel. Sadly, however, instead
of learning the lessons of the Exodus, Israel had begun to emulate
the Egyptian society they were instructed to reject.

SHLOMO'S RELATIONSHIP WITH GOD FRACTURED

In the following chapter of Melakhim, God appears to Shlomo in
another dream. At first God confirmed that He had heard Shlomo's
prayer and acknowledged that He would reside in the Temple forever. But again, as in Shlomo's last prophecy, God presented His
commitment to Shlomo as conditional. Yet now cracks had begun
to appear in the relationship between Shlomo and God,[11] for this
time the prophecy even included a warning of what would happen
if the commandments were not kept:

---

11. Yehuda Kiel, *Daat Mikra: Melakhim* (Jerusalem: Mossad Harav Kook, 1989), 201.

> As for you – if you walk before Me as your father David did, whole-heartedly and sincerely fulfilling all I have commanded you, and if you keep My laws and My rulings, then I will establish your royal throne over Israel forever, as I promised your father David: No one of your lineage will be cut off from the throne of Israel. But if you and your sons dare turn away from Me and do not keep the commandments and laws I set before you, and serve other gods and worship them, then I will cut Israel off from the face of the land that I gave them, and I will cast away from My presence the House I have sanctified for My name; and Israel will become but a proverb and a byword among all the nations. And whoever passes by this once-exalted House will reel and hiss and say, "Why did the Lord do such a thing to this land and this House?" and they will answer, "Because they left the Lord, their God, who brought their ancestors out of the land of Egypt, and they embraced other gods and worshipped them and served them. For this the Lord brought all this evil upon them." (Melakhim I 9:4–9)

Here, too, there is mention of Egypt, but the connotation is reversed. Instead of reveling in the history of God's redemption of Israel from Egypt as Shlomo did, God mentioned the redemption from Egypt as the justification for requiring Israel's obedience, and the subsequent punishment if the laws were not kept.

We repeatedly see a parallel between Israel and Egypt. This is not surprising, because for the first time in Israel's history a comparison between the two nations could be made. Israel had become a regional power, with massive building projects and a powerful monarch. In principle, these were all positive developments. A unified people, blessed with peace and prosperity, and a magnificent Temple for God had been the nation of Israel's goals for centuries.

However, there were significant dangers if Israel became like Egypt. In fact, according to many opinions, the Torah does not even command that Israel appoint a king,[12] even though without a strong monarchy the permanent Temple might never have been built. Instead, we see that appointing a king is dependent on the desire of the people to have one:

> When you enter the land that the Lord your God is giving you, and have taken possession of it and settled in it, should you say, "I will set a king over me, like all the surrounding nations," set over you a king whom the Lord your God chooses. The king you set over you must be one of your own people. You may not set a foreigner over you, who is not your brother. (Devarim 17:14–15)

Yet even after the king is appointed, there are limitations on him – unparalleled at that time in history:

> Further, he must not acquire many horses for himself, he must not make the people return to Egypt to acquire more horses, since the Lord has told you: "You must not go back that way again." He must not accumulate wives and let his heart be led astray, nor should he amass large amounts of silver and gold. (Devarim 17:16–17)

Note that here, too, Egypt is mentioned – it is forbidden for the nation to return to Egypt. But we see that as time passed, Shlomo yielded to the temptations of the throne and violated each of these restrictions. Despite the prohibition against amassing silver and gold, he possessed unparalleled quantities (Melakhim I 10:14–21).

---

12. See R. Nehorai's opinion in Sanhedrin 20b; Abrabanel on Devarim 17:14; Ibn Ezra on Devarim 17:15.

He ignored the proscription against keeping many horses, and notably acquired them from Egypt (Melakhim I 10:26–29).

Finally, Shlomo violated the restriction on the number of wives, and as predicted, they led his heart astray:[13]

> King Shlomo loved many foreign women besides the daughter of Pharaoh[14] – Moabite women, Amonite women, Edomite women, Sidonian women, Hittite women – from the nations of which the Lord had warned the Israelites: "You must not join with them, nor must they join with you, for they will turn your hearts astray after their own gods." Shlomo clung to these in love. He had seven hundred wives of royal rank and three hundred concubines, and his wives turned his heart astray. By the time Shlomo grew old, his wives had turned his heart to other gods, and his heart was not entirely with the Lord, his God, as his father David's heart had been. Shlomo went after Ashtoret, the god of the Sidonians, and after Milkom, the abomination of the Amonites. Shlomo did what was evil in the Lord's sight and was not fully with the Lord, as his father David was. It was then that Shlomo built a high shrine to Kemosh, the abomination of Moav, on the hill overlooking Jerusalem, and to Molekh, the abomination of the Amonites. He did

---

13. A daring midrash brought by Rashi in his commentary on Melakhim I 10:13 says Shlomo's earlier encounter with the Queen of Sheva led to the future birth of Nevukhadnetzar, who destroyed the very Temple that Shlomo built. While the text of Melakhim does not indicate any physical relationship between Shlomo and the queen, the Sages certainly picked up on the problematic nature of Shlomo's relationships with foreign women. See also Sanhedrin 21b for a midrash that connects Rome's eventual conquest of Israel with Shlomo's marriage to the daughter of Pharaoh.

14. While there was no criticism mentioned when Shlomo's marriage to Pharaoh's daughter first appeared in Melakhim I, 3, her inclusion in this list retroactively casts a shadow on what first appeared as a savvy diplomatic achievement.

the same for all his foreign wives, who offered incense and sacrifices to their gods. (Melakhim I 11:1–8)

There is a sharp contrast between Shlomo's love of foreign women here and Shlomo's love of God in Melakhim I 3:3.[15] He "clung to" and "loved" these women – a formula found in the commandments regarding our devotion to God (Devarim 11:22, 30:20). Shlomo's heart had long since forsaken its earlier devotion to God. The special relationship he had with God demanded loyalty, and once that loyalty was gone, their relationship could not be repaired.

God had warned Shlomo multiple times about his failure to follow the commandments, and his punishment was quick to come:

> Then the Lord raged against Shlomo, for his heart had turned away from the Lord, God of Israel, who had appeared to him twice and commanded him about this very matter – not to follow after other gods. But he failed to keep the Lord's command. And the Lord said to Shlomo, "Because this has been your will, and you failed to keep My covenant and My laws, which I commanded you – I will surely tear the kingdom away from you, and I will give it to your servant.[16] But for the sake of your father David, I will not do this in your own lifetime; I will tear it away from the hand of your son. And even so, I will not tear the whole kingdom away; I will grant a single tribe to your son for the sake of My servant David and for the sake of Jerusalem, which I have chosen." (Melakhim I 11:9–13)

---

15. Kiel, *Daat Mikra: Melakhim*, 45–46.
16. This fulfills the promise made in Melakhim I 3:14, where God makes Shlomo's success conditional on his following God's edicts: "And if you follow in My ways and keep My laws and commandments...."

Immediately following this, we read of various foreign adversaries that rose up against Shlomo, culminating in the rebellion of Yorovam, one of Shlomo's own servants.[17] The last verse before Shlomo's death describes his pursuit of Yorovam.[18]

Early in his reign, Shlomo ignored the warning in the book of Devarim against reliance on Egypt and tried to advance political and economic goals by marrying Pharaoh's daughter. However, in the end, his enemy took refuge in Egypt:

וַיְבַקֵּשׁ שְׁלֹמֹה לְהָמִית אֶת־יָרָבְעָם וַיָּקָם יָרָבְעָם וַיִּבְרַח מִצְרַיִם אֶל־שִׁישַׁק מֶלֶךְ־מִצְרַיִם וַיְהִי בְמִצְרַיִם עַד־מוֹת שְׁלֹמֹה:

Shlomo **sought** to put Yorovam to death, but Yorovam **fled** straight to Egypt, to King Shishak of Egypt, and he remained in Egypt until Shlomo's death. (Melakhim I 11:40)

This verse has strong parallels to a verse in Shemot:

וַיִּשְׁמַע פַּרְעֹה אֶת־הַדָּבָר הַזֶּה וַיְבַקֵּשׁ לַהֲרֹג אֶת־מֹשֶׁה וַיִּבְרַח מֹשֶׁה מִפְּנֵי פַרְעֹה וַיֵּשֶׁב בְּאֶרֶץ־מִדְיָן וַיֵּשֶׁב עַל־הַבְּאֵר:

Word reached Pharaoh and he **sought** to kill Moshe. But Moshe **fled** his presence and went to live in the land of Midyan. There he sat down beside a well. (Shemot 2:15)

Just as Pharaoh sought to kill the fleeing Moshe, Shlomo sought to kill the fleeing Yorovam.[19] Like a classical tragedy, we see the final downfall of Shlomo – he had become like Pharaoh. As narrated in the book of Shemot, the exodus from Egypt was the foundational

---

17. Melakhim I 11:14–40.
18. Ibid., v. 40.
19. Just as after Pharaoh died, Moshe could return to Egypt (Shemot 4:19), after Shlomo died, Yorovam could return from Egypt (Melakhim I 12:2–3).

event of the people of Israel. However, in Shlomo's time, we find the opposite recounted in the book of Melakhim: Instead of Israel leaving Egypt, Israel had come to mirror the same Egypt we were commanded to reject.

Although David, Shlomo's father, had also sinned, he otherwise always remained loyal to God: "For David had done what was right in the eyes of the Lord and never turned away from all He commanded him throughout his life – except in the matter of Uriya the Hittite" (Melakhim I 15:5).

There is no comparison between David and Pharaoh or Israel and Egypt during King David's reign. When David sinned, he confessed and repented (Shmuel II 12:13). Shlomo was instructed to be like his father, and did not succeed.[20] In the end, there is no sign of Shlomo repenting, and as we shall see, there is evidence that instead of confessing his sins, he rationalized them. God has patience for those who give in to their evil inclination and sin, if they repent. But rationalizations, which justify the rebellious behavior as normative, preclude any such repentance; in these cases, God is much less likely to forgive. As we shall see, this is a major lesson taught in Kohelet.

---

20. David's faithfulness to God is reflected in the fact that he is called a "servant of God" (Shmuel II 3:18; Melakhim I 3:6; Yeḥezkel 34:23; Tehillim 18:1, 36:1), a phrase applied to no other biblical figures except Moshe and Yehoshua. The Midrash (*Sifrei Vaetḥanan* 27 on Devarim 3:24) notes there are those whom God called His servants, and those who called themselves God's servants. David fits in both categories. Shlomo is in the group of those who called themselves God's servants (Melakhim I 3:9), but God never called Shlomo His servant. The Midrash notes that when addressing Shlomo, God always referenced his father David as His servant. This emphasizes the essential difference in the relationships of David and Shlomo to God.

Chapter 2

Shlomo's Life in the Book of Kohelet

KOHELET DISCUSSES SHLOMO'S YOUTH

Throughout the book of Kohelet, we find verses that allude to various stages of Shlomo's story that enumerate his regrets about his life. While we read about Shlomo's failings on a political and personal level that occurred later in his life, there are some verses that hearken back to his youth, at the beginning of his reign: "Better a good name than good oil; better the day of death than the day of birth" (Kohelet 7:1). Shlomo says that a good name is better than good oil. What name and what oil is he referring to?

As we saw earlier, after Shlomo's birth, God gave him the name Yedidya (Shmuel II 12:25). It is rare for God to give names to people in the Tanakh, and the name God bestowed on Shlomo illustrates His particular love for him. It literally means "beloved of God" (and shares the same Hebrew root as "David," Shlomo's father, who also had a special relationship with God).

The "good oil" in this verse refers to the oil used to anoint kings.[1] Shlomo is reflecting on these two pivotal events in his youth – receiving a name from God and becoming king. From the perspective of the end of his life (near the "day of death"), he realizes it would have been better to have remained just God's beloved, and never to have become king – since his position as king eventually led to the rupture in his relationship with God.

> Young man, rejoice now in your youth; let your heart give you pleasure while you are young. Follow your heart where it leads you, your eyes where they allure you – and know that God will bring you to judgment for all this. (Kohelet 11:9)

Shlomo is thinking back to his younger self and giving retroactive advice. He knows that at that age, it is natural to enjoy life. But there is a cost to following one's "heart and eyes" (we will see the significance of this later), for in the end, God will execute judgment (*mishpat*). The judgment of God mentioned here is presented as a contrast to Shlomo's judgment of the two women in Melakhim I 3:28. While there the nation "heard of the judgment which the king had judged, and they feared the king," Shlomo in his own life did not display the same fear of God who would ultimately judge him.

Another verse in Kohelet also relates to that judgment: "I said in my heart: God will judge both the righteous and the wicked, for the time will come for every deed, for all that is done there" (Kohelet 3:17).

Kohelet is saying that God determines who is righteous and who is wicked.[2] While Shlomo did execute justice with wisdom

---

1. Targum and Seforno on Kohelet 7:1.
2. Mordekhai Zer-Kavod, "Kohelet," in *Daat Mikra: Hamesh Megillot* (Jerusalem: Mossad Harav Kook, 1990), Kohelet 3:17.

in the case of the two women, that wisdom was granted him by God. Ultimately, the real judgment should be attributed to God.

Preceding this famous judgment, Shlomo had the equally famous dream where he asked God for the wisdom to distinguish "between good and bad" (Melakhim I 3:9), and received in return not only wisdom, but also "wealth and honor – not a man among kings will compare to you for as long as you live" (3:13). This was a moment of great closeness between Shlomo and God.

But at the end of his life, Shlomo has less affinity for dreams. He says his dreams did not lead to anything positive. He should have simply feared God: "For so many dreams are so much empty breath, so many words – better only to fear God" (Kohelet 5:6). Likewise: "For as dreams come with too much preoccupation, so is a fool's speech known by too many words" (5:2).

Shlomo's dream in which he received wisdom also came with "much preoccupation." But in the end, by not fearing God, even Shlomo, the "wisest of all men," feels like a fool, whose speech is nothing but empty words.

The idea that Shlomo saw himself as a fool in his youth is evident in yet another verse in Kohelet: "Better to heed the rebuke of the wise than to hear the song of fools. For fools' cackling is like the crackling of thorns under the pot. That too is empty breath" (7:5–6).

Shlomo recognizes that it can be uncomfortable to listen to reproof, and it would be more pleasant to hear the song of fools. But he must let his readers know the truth. Perhaps in his analogy of the "crackling of thorns under the pot," *hasirim taḥat hasir,* there is a veiled reference to a work that Shlomo wrote in his youth – Shir HaShirim. By the end of his life, did Shlomo view the youthful optimism of Shir HaShirim as the "song of fools"?

KOHELET ON BUILDING THE TEMPLE
AND OPPRESSING THE PEOPLE

The next verse leads into the subsequent phase of Shlomo's life:

כִּי הָעֹשֶׁק יְהוֹלֵל חָכָם וִיאַבֵּד אֶת־לֵב מַתָּנָה.

For oppression makes the wise man foolish and a gift
destroys the heart. (Kohelet 7:7)

If we previously saw that Shlomo felt he had been a fool earlier
in life, how do we understand his transformation back into a fool
in light of God's granting him wisdom? Shlomo's answer here is
"oppression." When he began to oppress the people during his
reign,[3] he turned from a wise man into a foolish one. The second
half of the verse alludes to how he initially received the wisdom.
While the translation here is "a gift destroys the heart" (likely
referring to bribes), the literal reading could be "he will lose the
heart gift." This hints to Melakhim I 3:12, where God "gave him a
wise and understanding heart." Now Shlomo laments losing that
divine gift.

Why does oppression cause the heart to be lost? Because one
of the commandments for the king is "to not act haughtily to his
brothers" – לְבִלְתִּי רוּם־לְבָבוֹ מֵאֶחָיו (Devarim 17:20). However, the
literal meaning of that phrase is "to not raise his heart above his
brothers."

When Shlomo asked God for wisdom, he referred to himself as
"Your servant … among Your people" (Melakhim I 3:8). He hum-
bly understood that even though he was king, he was one of the
people. In response, God gave Shlomo a heart to promote justice
among those people. But when Shlomo oppressed the people, and
lifted his heart above them, the divine gift did not fulfill its purpose.

---

3. See examples of Shlomo's oppression of the people (for example, by forced labor)
   above, on pp. 9–10.

Therefore, in Kohelet, Shlomo describes his kingdom as a place of oppression. His capital, Jerusalem, which should have been a place of justice and righteousness, had become a place of wickedness: "Another thing that I saw beneath the sun: in the place of justice – there is wickedness; where righteousness is – wickedness is there" (Kohelet 3:16).

Instead of comforting the oppressed with righteous justice, Shlomo became the oppressor: "I turned again and saw all those oppressed beneath the sun. There they were: the tears of the oppressed and none to console them; power in the hands of their oppressors and none to console them" (4:1).

But now, at the end of his life, Shlomo knows that even though he oppressed people in his kingdom, there is a higher One, God, who watches over everyone: "If you see oppression of a poor person or any perversion of law and justice in the province, do not wonder at the fact, for there is One higher than high who watches, with high ones above them" (5:7).

Why did Shlomo oppress the people? Ostensibly, for a noble purpose – he wanted to build the Temple as a house for God. But the ends did not justify the means, for above all, God wants man to follow His laws: "Watch your step when you go to the House of God. Better to hearken than to bring the offering of fools, for they do not know they are doing evil" (4:17).

Once again, Shlomo sees himself as a fool for not listening to God. He was so eager to build the Temple that he ignored the objective of the entire project.[4]

The emphasis on obedience over the sacrificial service is also found in the story of Sha'ul, the first king of Israel. Sha'ul also

---

4. Even before building the Temple, it is recorded that Shlomo "offered a thousand burnt offerings" in Givon (Melakhim I 3:4). These thousand offerings parallel his thousand wives. The latter thousand is a sign of disobedience, and God prefers obedience to sacrifice, no matter how copious.

thought sacrifice was more important than following the command of God, and the prophet Shmuel castigated him:

> Does the Lord delight in burnt offerings and sacrifices as much as obedience to the Lord's voice? Behold – obedience is better than sacrifice, and compliance than the fat of rams. For rebellion is as bad as the sin of divination, and defiance as corruption and idolatry. Because you rejected the word of the Lord, He has rejected you as king. (Shmuel I 15:22–23)

Just like Sha'ul,[5] Shlomo ended up rejected by God, with his kingdom torn away from him. This sad outcome is reflected in this verse in Kohelet: "He who quarries stones will be hurt by them; he who chops trees will be harmed by them" (Kohelet 10:9).

In building the Temple, Shlomo used stones (Melakhim I 5:31)[6] and trees (5:20). In the end, not only did the people suffer, but Shlomo was hurt by the project as well. The heavy, forced labor that came with the obsessive building led the people to resent his rule, and eventually reject it.

KOHELET ON SHLOMO'S VIOLATIONS OF THE LAWS OF KINGS

Beyond the general wrong of oppressing the people, we saw earlier that Shlomo was guilty of violating explicit prohibitions related

---

5. Kohelet Rabba explains the verse, "So do not be too righteous..." (Kohelet 7:16) as applying to Sha'ul in this story. Sha'ul had mercy on Agag, king of the nation of Amalek, and in effect tried "to be more righteous than the Creator" (See also Yoma 22b and Targum on Kohelet 2:15). Rationalizing violation of God's commandments is unacceptable, even for reasons of righteousness, and certainly not for a king, who represents the entire nation in their relationship to God.

6. The only biblical mentions of quarrying stones are these two verses in Melakhim and Kohelet. Therefore, the negative connotation in Kohelet can be applied to Shlomo's building project in Melakhim as well.

to the king: not to amass gold and horses, and not to marry many wives. These appear in Kohelet as well.

In chapter 2, Kohelet describes his accomplishments. The verses apply fittingly to Shlomo:

הִגְדַּלְתִּי מַעֲשָׂי בָּנִיתִי לִי בָּתִּים נָטַעְתִּי לִי כְּרָמִים:

I **increased** my possessions. I built myself houses and I planted vineyards. (Kohelet 2:4)[7]

Melakhim I 7:1–12 states that Shlomo built houses, and Shir HaShirim 8:11 mentions Shlomo's vineyard. While these possessions are legitimate,[8] the book of Kohelet describes more problematic acquisitions:

> I bought slaves and maidservants, and others were born in my house; I had livestock also, herds and flocks, more than anyone else who came before me in Jerusalem. I collected silver and gold and the treasures of kings and foreign lands; I brought in singers, male and female, and all the delights of mankind – chests and chests [*shida veshidot*] of them. (Kohelet 2:7–8)

---

7. Thomas Krüger (*Qoheleth: A Commentary* [Minneapolis: Fortress Press, 2004], 66) observes that even the verb construct (*binyan*) in this verse is significant: "If according to [Melakhim I] 1:37 and 47 God made Solomon's throne great (גדל *gdl piel* [the active or intensive construct]), here King [Kohelet] *himself* makes his works great (גדל *gdl hiphil* [the causative construct])."

8. However, Radiša Antic (p. 8) notes that in these verses, by describing the activities and possessions of Shlomo, Kohelet is "referring to the mindset of [Kayin, who performed similar achievements], as opposed to that of Hevel [who had no successors or legacy]." By associating himself with Kayin, Shlomo may be expressing regret for even these permitted actions. See Radiša Antic, "Cain, Abel, Seth, and the Meaning of Human Life as Portrayed in the Books of Genesis and Ecclesiastes," in *Andrews University Seminary Studies* 44.2 (2006): 210.

In addition to the slaves – a sign of his oppression of the people[9] – Shlomo also boasts about how much gold he had, despite the prohibition. Verse 8 also has the unusual phrase *shida veshidot*, translated here as "chests and chests," although other translations fit better with the above prohibitions.[10]

How did Shlomo, the wisest of men, come to violate such explicit prohibitions? The Talmud explains:

> And R. Yitzhak says: For what reason were the rationales of Torah commandments not revealed? It was because the rationales of two verses were revealed, and the greatest in the world [King Shlomo] failed in those matters. It is written with regard to a king: "He shall not add many wives for himself, that his heart should not turn away" (Devarim 17:17). Shlomo said: "I will add many, but I will not turn away." And later, it is written: "In his old age, his wives turned away Shlomo's heart after other gods" (Melakhim I 11:4). And it is also written: "Only he shall not accumulate many horses for himself nor return the people to Egypt for the sake of accumulating horses" (Devarim 17:16), and Shlomo said: "I will accumulate many, but I will not return."

---

9. While slavery was a common practice at that time, Shlomo's reign was supposed to be the pinnacle of the process that began with the exodus from Egypt. To have the Temple built on the backs of slaves (as opposed to the Tabernacle in the time of Moshe, which was constructed in a voluntary, public effort) was a sign of oppression.

10. Ibn Ezra says it means "women," and modern commentaries such as Gordis concur (see Robert Gordis, *Koheleth· The Man and His World – A Study of Ecclesiastes* [New York: Schocken Press, 1968]). If this is true, then Shlomo is mentioning his vast number of wives. Rashi says it refers to carriages, and Zer-Kavod in *Daat Mikra*, following Rashi's interpretation, points out that these carriages, hitched to horses, allude to Shlomo's massive stables of horses.

Another verse in Kohelet that hints to Shlomo's seven hundred wives and three hundred concubines is 7:28, where we read, "I found one in a thousand." While the plain meaning of the text refers to finding an upright person, Zer-Kavod points out that by using that specific number, it is alluding to Shlomo's one thousand women.

And it is written: "And a chariot came up and went out of Egypt for six hundred shekels of silver." (Melakhim I 10:29)[11]

When Shlomo saw the purpose for those prohibitions, he rationalized his violations by saying the end result wouldn't apply to him.[12] He would not turn away; he would not return to Egypt. In the end, not only did he not demonstrate the required obedience to God inherent in the very concept of divine commandments, but those same predictions also came true: His wives did lead him astray, and he did send his merchants to Egypt.

In Kohelet, we see the consequences of that rationalization:

יָדַעְתִּי כִּי כָּל־אֲשֶׁר יַעֲשֶׂה הָאֱלֹהִים הוּא יִהְיֶה לְעוֹלָם עָלָיו אֵין לְהוֹסִיף וּמִמֶּנּוּ אֵין לִגְרֹעַ וְהָאֱלֹהִים עָשָׂה שֶׁיִּרְאוּ מִלְּפָנָיו.

And I know that whatever God has made will exist forever. **There is no adding to it, there is no taking away;** and God has made quite sure that He be feared. (Kohelet 3:14)

Shlomo realizes that God's commandments are meant to apply eternally, and the negative consequences for violating them are unavoidable. The verse uses the same language as this warning in the Torah:

אֵת כָּל־הַדָּבָר אֲשֶׁר אָנֹכִי מְצַוֶּה אֶתְכֶם אֹתוֹ תִשְׁמְרוּ לַעֲשׂוֹת לֹא־תֹסֵף עָלָיו וְלֹא תִגְרַע מִמֶּנּוּ:

Beware: fulfill all that I command you. **Neither add to it nor take away from it.** (Devarim 13:1)

---

11. Sanhedrin 21b.
12. Rabbi Yosef Kara, in his commentary on Kohelet 7:16, says that the words "do not be excessively wise" refer to Shlomo's rationalization of his defiance of these commandments.

The Torah is telling us that we need to remain obedient to the commandments of God because He gave them to us, and Kohelet explains that God made humans so they would fear and obey Him. Even if we start out with good intentions, the law must be obeyed. Corruption, both personal and political, occurs when a person convinces himself that a goal – personal or public – outweighs the law. The law is there to prevent this corruption, which might start out high minded, but which quickly deteriorates to personal benefit.[13] Shlomo thought that for diplomatic and military reasons he could violate the laws against marrying foreign women and amassing too many horses, but in the end, the failures became entirely personal.

KOHELET ON THE OUTCOME OF SHLOMO'S FAILINGS

As we saw earlier, Shlomo's punishment for his failure to obey God and His commands was the same as Sha'ul's punishment: having the kingdom torn away from him. When Sha'ul received this message from the prophet Shmuel, he begged that the decree be canceled, only to be told that God "will not lie nor change his mind: for He is not a man, that He should change His mind" (Shmuel I 15:29). No such incident is told regarding Shlomo, although perhaps a verse in Kohelet alludes to it: "Do not take flight – walk clear away; do not persist in an evil thing, for he will do what it pleases him to do" (Kohelet 8:3).

Based on the previous verse ("Obey the king's word, I say, and the word of your oath to God"), this verse is discussing how to relate to a king. The second half of the verse should be understood as "Don't stand in penitence and beg that the king rescind

---

13. This is analogous to the speed limit today. People might think they can drive safely above the speed limit, and they have important reasons to do so. But once they don't recognize that the law applies to them, they will do it even when it is not justified.

his harsh decree, for there is no hope he will change his mind, as he will do anything he pleases."[14]

Perhaps Shlomo, knowing the lesson of Sha'ul, did not even try to convince God to rescind His decree; or, like Sha'ul, Shlomo (in an unrecorded story) also begged for a reprieve, but learned that God, the King of kings, would not change His mind.[15]

Not only did God say He would tear the kingdom away from Shlomo, but He also added that He would "give it to one of your servants." Several verses in Kohelet refer to this future, where slaves[16] replace their masters: "I have seen slaves riding on horseback and princes walking like slaves upon the ground" (Kohelet 10:7). Here we see slaves riding on those very horses that were symbols of royalty,[17] and those who formerly held power now reduced to walking on foot.

In another excerpt, Kohelet mentions a slave cursing him: "Also, do not pay attention to everything that is said; do not listen to your slave when he curses you. For many times, as your heart well knows, you yourself have cursed others" (7:21–22). This could be a reference to Yorovam, who was a servant of Shlomo's and rebelled against him (Melakhim I 11:26). But when did Shlomo curse others?

---

14. Zer-Kavod in *Daat Mikra* on Kohelet 8:3, after reviewing and rejecting alternate commentaries.

15. As we noted earlier, God forgave David for his sins, but did not do the same for his predecessor Sha'ul or for successor Shlomo. This may be attributed to the fact that David sinned in a grave manner, but never ignored God's command to him. His continued faithfulness made his repentance genuine, whereas when Sha'ul and Shlomo decided that God's rules did not apply to them, they fractured the framework of their relationship with God in such a way that God could not accept any requests for mercy. In Shlomo's case, God even says that only for David's sake did He not depose Shlomo in his lifetime.

16. Or servants; the same Hebrew word, *eved*, is used for both.

17. And of royal corruption as well, considering the prohibition forbidding the king to both amass horses and import them from Egypt.

This might refer to the case of Shimi ben Gera, who had tormented Shlomo's father, David. After Shlomo became king, Shlomo forbade Shimi from leaving Jerusalem. When a few years later Shimi did leave the city, Shlomo condemned him:

> The king sent and summoned Shimi and said to him, "Did I not make you swear[18] to the Lord and warn you that from the moment you left and went anywhere else, you would know that you would be doomed to death? And you said to me, 'Very well, I accept.' Why did you fail to keep the Lord's oath and the command I charged you with?" The king then continued to Shimi, "You are aware of all the evil you harbored in your heart; of what you did to my father David. Now the Lord has brought your own evil back on your own head." (Melakhim I 2:42–44)

Shlomo was angry with Shimi for not listening to his commandment and determined that he should be punished. And God cursed Shlomo for the same reason. Only at the end of his life, in the book of Kohelet, does Shlomo recognize the irony of cursing Shimi for a lack of obedience when he himself had the same failing. Just as Shimi walked away from Jerusalem in defiance of the king's command, so too did Shlomo go (literally, "walked")[19] after other gods. God's condemnation of Shlomo uses similar language to the curse Shlomo uses against Shimi: Both violators are accused of not keeping the commandment they had been given.

SHLOMO'S LEGACY IS FRAGMENTED

Another verse shows that the fortunes of a king can be reversed:

---

18. Radak points out (in the name of his father) that while there is no mention of Shimi taking an oath to Shlomo, we learn from Kohelet that a king's command is like an oath: "Keep the king's command, and in the manner of an oath of God" (8:2).
19. Melakhim I 11:5, 10.

> Better a poor but clever youth than an old and foolish king, who does not know how to take heed anymore. For [the youth] may come out of a dungeon to become king, but [the king] born to royalty can become poor. (Kohelet 4:13–14)

Shlomo is looking back on his kingship, and realizes that when he reached adulthood, he should have been more careful. Despite being renowned for his wisdom, he acted like a fool. And now Yorovam, a young man born of low status who deserved to be imprisoned (in "a dungeon") for rebelling against Shlomo, will come to be king of northern Israel instead of Reḥavam– who was "born to kingship."[20]

The following verses provide one more example of a stranger taking what should have been Shlomo's legacy to his future descendants:

> There is an evil I have seen beneath the sun, and the harm it does people is great. There will be a man to whom God gives wealth, possessions, and honor so that he lacks nothing his heart desires. And then God will not grant him the power to partake of it, and a stranger will consume it all; this is futility and an evil sickness. (6:1–2)

Shlomo received God's gift of prosperity[21] and built the Temple. Ideally, his descendants would have happily enjoyed this

---

20. There seems to be a contradiction between this verse, which praises a young king, and Kohelet 10:16: "I pity you, the land whose king is a lad." However, it appears that the latter verse is referring to Shlomo himself as a young king (as he called himself in Melakhim I 3:7). A hint to this can be found in the next verse, which lauds kings who avoid drunkenness. As we shall see, there are several sources that associate Shlomo's rule with excessive drinking of wine.

21. The phrase used to describe prosperity granted by God here – "wealth, possessions, and honor" – is found identically in the description of God's response to Shlomo's request for wisdom in Divrei HaYamim II 1:11–12.

idyllic situation for generations. But due to Shlomo's failings, a stranger – Yorovam – would control much more of the kingdom than Shlomo's son Reḥavam would.

Moreover, Shlomo is not happy about Reḥavam inheriting the kingdom from him.[22] He had built up an empire, and was frustrated to foresee the foolishness of his son Reḥavam[23] leading to the collapse of such a monumental undertaking:

> And I hated all the labor I had labored beneath the sun; all to be left to some person who will come after me. Who knows whether he will be wise or foolish; either way, he will control all that I toiled for wisely beneath the sun; that too is futile. (2:18–19)

Shlomo was wise, the wisest of men, but through his sin, so much potential good was lost. This feeling of regret over what might have been, what should have been, is summed up thus: "Better wisdom than weaponry, but one sinner destroys much good" (9:18).

Through his wisdom, Shlomo was able to achieve unprecedented peace for Israel; but through his sins, all of that was destroyed.

---

22. See Targum on Kohelet, who explains the ensuing verses as referring to Shlomo's contemplating Reḥavam's future reign.
23. See Melakhim I 12:1–16, where Reḥavam ignored the wise advice of the elders and increased his oppression of the people, which led to the division of his kingdom.

Section Two

Kohelet and Bereshit

Chapter 3

Adam as Kohelet

WHOM IS SHLOMO THINKING ABOUT?

As noted above,[1] Kohelet is traditionally attributed to Shlomo at the end of his life. After having gone from an early life imbued with love of God and the divine promise of a reign of unmatched wealth and success, only to end with disgrace and God's castigation, he certainly looked back with regret over how he arrived at this low point.[2]

Looking back in history, Shlomo would find one person whose path most closely resembled his own: Adam. As the first human, Adam represents all humanity,[3] and through his reputation,

---

1. P. 3.
2. The Talmud (Sanhedrin 20b; Gittin 68b; Megilla 11b) and Midrash (*Kohelet Rabba* 1:12) go even further than the biblical text, and claim that as a result of his failings, Shlomo was deposed. According to some opinions, he did not end his life as king. The basis of these midrashim is Kohelet 1:12, where Kohelet states, "I, Kohelet, *was* king of Israel in Jerusalem" – the past tense implying that at the time of the writing, he was no longer king.
3. Adam's name became the name for all future humans. Thus, aspects of his life have universal resonance.

Shlomo was the first representative of Israel to be universally known. The entire known world was in Adam's dominion, and Shlomo could acquire whatever he desired, from anywhere; no figure in the history of the nation had such a universal scope.

Both Adam and Shlomo started out with enormous potential and a unique relationship with God. Both desired knowledge, both had wives that "led them astray" (although the ultimate responsibility for their failings was their own), and both experienced a form of exile from God's special place: Adam was expelled from the Garden, while Shlomo abandoned the Temple of God[4] and strayed to the shrines of Khemosh and Molekh.[5]

Shlomo identified with Adam's life, and so he wrote Kohelet in a way that reflected both Adam's life and his own. By writing as Adam, Shlomo shows that nothing has changed; the downfall of man has existed since the very beginning. The opening chapter of Kohelet is dedicated to this concept:

> What has been is what will be, what was done will again be done, and there is nothing new under the sun.[6] Something may make a person say, "Look at this: it is new!" – it already existed in all the eons that came before us. (Kohelet 1:9–10)

This idea is repeated later in the book: "Do not say, 'What happened, that times gone by were better than these?' It is not wisdom

---

4. In chapter 17, we will discuss the parallels between the Garden and the Sanctuary.
5. Melakhim I 11:7.
6. The phrase "under the sun" appears many times in Kohelet. It refers specifically to the limited facilities of man, as opposed to the infinite power of God. The division between man on earth and God in heaven also appears in Kohelet 5:1, "For God is in heaven while you are here on earth." It is also noteworthy that all of the uses in the Torah of the related phrase "under the heavens" describe scenarios where God is or will be wiping out human lives (Bereshit 6:17 [Bereshit 1:9 is related to this verse]; Shemot 17:14; Devarim 7:24, 9:14, 25:19, 29:19). These verses therefore also emphasize the vulnerability of man in his relationship to God.

that leads you to ask" (7:10). Shlomo knows he was not the first to suffer from these mistakes; they go all the way back to Adam.

HOW DOES KOHELET ALLUDE TO ADAM?

Kohelet can be read as Adam reflecting back on the tragedies of his life. As such, which misfortunes would certainly be included? Surely the sin of eating the fruit with the consequent expulsion from Eden; and one son, Kayin, murdering the other, Hevel. The two are closely related, certainly in Adam's view. He searched after knowledge (eating from the Tree of Knowledge) instead of fearing God, and that led to the introduction of death into the world. These themes are found both in the Garden story and in the book of Kohelet.

In the Garden, the snake made grandiose promises: "But the snake told the woman, 'You will not die; God knows that on the day you eat from it your eyes will be opened, and you will be like God, knowing good and bad'" (Bereshit 3:4–5). He told the humans they would not die, but his lie was exposed when death was introduced to the world because of their actions. Consequently, the inevitability of death is one of the main themes of Kohelet.[7] The snake also promised them Godlike knowledge.[8] After eating from the tree, their eyes did open, but humans never acquired that divine level of knowledge. Kohelet likewise describes the futility of the search for wisdom.

Who was the first to die as a result of his sin? Adam's son Hevel. Therefore, the word *hevel* is repeated frequently throughout the book of Kohelet,[9] as if Adam is bemoaning his dead son, and the

---

7. See David M. Clemens, "The Law of Sin and Death: Ecclesiastes and Genesis 1–3" in *Themelios* 19.3 (1994), 7.
8. Rashi and Ibn Ezra on Bereshit 3:5. For an exploration of whether or not the snake was lying, see Jonathan Grossman, *Creation: The Story of Beginnings*, (Jerusalem: Maggid Books, 2019), 126.
9. As noted by the Gaon of Vilna in his commentary on Kohelet 1:1.

events that led to that tragedy. As one scholar put it, "If we were reading [Kohelet] as a narrative, we would conclude that [Hevel] is the main character of the story, the other main character being Adam."[10]

Adam also needed to work hard after leaving Eden. Kohelet repeatedly uses the word *amal*, which means work or labor, but which also has connotations of sin and suffering.[11]

Lastly, seeing the righteous Hevel die before the brother who murdered him, Adam must have wondered why things should be this way. And throughout Kohelet we find the ancient question repeated over and over: Why do the righteous suffer and the wicked prosper?

All this together paints a dark picture, but it does allow the book of Kohelet to relate to a story. It also makes the last two verses of Kohelet (12:13–14), which instruct the reader to "fear God and keep His commandments," much less jarring. On the face of it, these last verses seemed to be addressed to the Jewish nation in particular, as they are the only ones who have received divine commandments. But understanding the connection to Adam (whom God also commanded), allows them to fit into the general narrative of the book. They were not added on at the last minute to negate any problematic content found earlier, but rather are the pinnacle the author was working toward the entire time:

> The final word: it has all been said. Fear God and keep His commandments! For this is the whole of man [*adam*].[12] For

---

10. Brian G. Toews, "The Story of Abel: The Narrative Substructure of Ecclesiastes" (paper presented at the ETS meeting, Nov. 2007): 9.

11. This is in contrast to the more common Hebrew root A-V-D, which also has the positive connotations associated with the service of God.

12. The word *adam*, man, is used overwhelmingly instead of the synonym *ish* throughout Kohelet (forty-three uses of *adam* and six of *ish*). This, too, supports the idea that the book is referring specifically to Adam the first human, and not to the generic "man." Raymond Moxham notes ("Qohelet's Fall: The Use of Genesis 2–4 in the Book of

God will bring every deed to judgment, even hidden ones, whether good or bad [bringing to mind the Tree of Knowledge of good and bad]. (12:13–14)

Adam is looking back, saying if he had feared God and followed that first commandment God gave him, none of this would have come to pass.

The order of the book of Kohelet does not parallel the linear story of Bereshit (from the Tree story to the expulsion to the Kayin and Hevel story), but I propose that this is the point of Kohelet; to give us the impression that life does not have a clear beginning and end, but rather that everything is circular.[13] It is a puzzle waiting to be reassembled.

Ecclesiastes" [Master's thesis, University of Otago, 2015]: 28) that while *adam* is certainly a very common word in the Tanakh, the chapters where it appears with the highest density (percentage of total words) are in the book of Kohelet and Bereshit 1–4.

13. The Midrash (*Kohelet Rabba* 1:12) explains why Kohelet 1:12 ("I, Kohelet, was king of Israel in Jerusalem") is not the opening verse of the book by pointing out that Kohelet is not written in chronological order. The *Torah Temima* commentary on this midrash says the author organized the content according to his feelings, as a stream of consciousness, rather than in a chronological order of events. This can help explain why there are parallels between verses in Kohelet and Bereshit, but they do not match Bereshit chronologically.

Chapter 4

Adam in the Garden of Eden

A review of the verses from Kohelet will show just how strong its connection is to the story of Adam. In my comments, I will present a conjecture as to how the book of Kohelet reflects Adam's feelings at the end of his life. To show the connections among the various parts of Adam's life, I will arrange the verses according to their parallels in Bereshit (as opposed to their order in Kohelet). The bold words in each column represent parallel language.

CREATION

<table>
<tr>
<td>

וַיִּבְרָא אֱלֹהִים אֶת־הָאָדָם
בְּצַלְמוֹ בְּצֶלֶם אֱלֹהִים בָּרָא
אֹתוֹ זָכָר וּנְקֵבָה בָּרָא אֹתָם.

So God **created** the man in His image, in the image of God He created him; male and female He created them. (Bereshit 1:27)

</td>
<td>

וּזְכֹר אֶת־**בּוֹרְאֶיךָ** בִּימֵי בְּחוּרֹתֶיךָ עַד אֲשֶׁר
לֹא־יָבֹאוּ יְמֵי הָרָעָה וְהִגִּיעוּ שָׁנִים אֲשֶׁר תֹּאמַר
אֵין־לִי בָהֶם חֵפֶץ.

And remember your **Creator** in these days of your youth before the days of despair, before years come when you shall say, "There is nothing here that I desire." (Kohelet 12:1)

</td>
</tr>
</table>

The root ברא (*bara*) appears in both verses. Adam, created by God, pines for the time when he had a good relationship with his Creator – before the "days of sorrow" after the sin and the expulsion.

PLANTING

<table>
<tr>
<td>

וַיֹּאמֶר אֱלֹהִים תַּדְשֵׁא הָאָרֶץ דֶּשֶׁא עֵשֶׂב
מַזְרִיעַ זֶרַע עֵץ פְּרִי עֹשֶׂה פְּרִי לְמִינוֹ
אֲשֶׁר זַרְעוֹ־בוֹ עַל־הָאָרֶץ וַיְהִי־כֵן. וַתּוֹצֵא
הָאָרֶץ דֶּשֶׁא עֵשֶׂב מַזְרִיעַ זֶרַע לְמִינֵהוּ
וְעֵץ עֹשֶׂה־פְּרִי אֲשֶׁר זַרְעוֹ־בוֹ לְמִינֵהוּ
וַיַּרְא אֱלֹהִים כִּי־טוֹב.

Then God said, "Let the earth produce vegetation: seed-bearing plants and **fruit trees** of all the kinds on earth that grow seed-bearing fruit." And so it was. The earth produced vegetation: plants bearing seeds, each of its kind, and **trees bearing fruit** containing seeds, each of its kind. And God saw: it was good. (Bereshit 1:11–12)

</td>
<td>

עָשִׂיתִי לִי **גַנּוֹת** וּפַרְדֵּסִים **וְנָטַעְתִּי**
בָהֶם עֵץ כָּל־פֶּרִי.

I made **gardens** and orchards for myself and **planted** them with **every kind of fruit tree**. (Kohelet 2:5)

</td>
</tr>
</table>

וַיִּטַּע יְהוָה אֱלֹהִים גַּן־בְּעֵדֶן מִקֶּדֶם וַיָּשֶׂם שָׁם אֶת־הָאָדָם אֲשֶׁר יָצָר.	טוֹב מִשְּׁנֵיהֶם אֵת אֲשֶׁר־עֲדֶן לֹא הָיָה אֲשֶׁר לֹא־רָאָה אֶת־הַמַּעֲשֶׂה הָרָע אֲשֶׁר נַעֲשָׂה תַּחַת הַשָּׁמֶשׁ.
The Lord God **planted** a **garden** in Eden, in the east, and there he put the man He had formed. (Bereshit 2:8)	But better than either are those who have not **yet** [*aden*] come into being, for they have seen none of the evil that is wrought beneath the sun. (Kohelet 4:3)

The verses in both Kohelet and Bereshit have planting, gardens, and trees. Particularly unique is the phrasing *etz... pri*, which appears only one other time in the entire Tanakh.[1]

The first Kohelet verse (2:5), which evokes God's creation of the world, uses verbs similar to those found in the Creation narrative. It appears in a section where the narrator describes everything he has accomplished: constructing pools of water and irrigating forests; acquiring slaves and servants, herds, and flocks; amassing treasures and other luxuries. Adam thought at first that his efforts would be as successful as those carried out by God in the Garden. But unlike God's gardens and trees, which last forever, in Kohelet 2:11, he admits that everything he did was futile. He constantly needed to start again:

> And then I turned to look at all my works, at the work of my hands, at all that I had labored to achieve – and this is what I saw: it was all futile, nothing but pursuit of wind, and there is no true profit beneath the sun.

The second Kohelet verse (4:3) uses a word for "yet" which only appears in the Tanakh there: *aden*.[2] It is strikingly similar to the word Eden and is in fact spelled the same way: עדן. Perhaps Adam

---

1. Tehillim 148:9.
2. In later rabbinic Hebrew, there is the more familiar *adayin*.

is saying it would have been better not to have been in Eden at all, "that Eden had not come into being."

BODIES OF WATER

וְנָהָר יֹצֵא מֵעֵדֶן לְהַשְׁקוֹת אֶת־הַגָּן וּמִשָּׁם יִפָּרֵד וְהָיָה לְאַרְבָּעָה רָאשִׁים.	כָּל־הַנְּחָלִים הֹלְכִים אֶל־הַיָּם וְהַיָּם אֵינֶנּוּ מָלֵא אֶל־מְקוֹם שֶׁהַנְּחָלִים הֹלְכִים שָׁם הֵם שָׁבִים לָלָכֶת.
A river flows from Eden to water the Garden, and from there divides into four headwaters. (Bereshit 2:10)	All streams flow into the sea, yet the sea is not full. To the places where the streams first flowed, they return to flow again. (Kohelet 1:7)

Unlike the streams that all flowed into the Garden, in the post-Eden world the streams flow into the sea, but it can never be filled. There used to be an objective to the flowing, but no longer.

GOD, MAN, AND EATING

וַיְצַו יְהוָה אֱלֹהִים עַל־הָאָדָם לֵאמֹר מִכֹּל עֵץ־הַגָּן אָכֹל תֹּאכֵל.	אֵין־טוֹב בָּאָדָם שֶׁיֹּאכַל וְשָׁתָה וְהֶרְאָה אֶת־נַפְשׁוֹ טוֹב בַּעֲמָלוֹ גַּם־זֹה רָאִיתִי אָנִי כִּי מִיַּד הָאֱלֹהִים הִיא.
And the Lord **God** commanded the **man**: "You are free to **eat** from any tree in the Garden." (Bereshit 2:16)	There is nothing better for a **man** to do than to **eat** and drink and reap some good from his labor; this too I saw comes from **God**. (Kohelet 2:24)

In both verses, we find God, man (*adam*), and eating. At the end of his life, Adam knows that all food "comes from God"; thus, he should not have eaten from the tree. He realizes he should have been satisfied with "every tree of the Garden," but his greed caused him to covet the one tree not allowed to him.[3]

כִּי מִי יֹאכַל וּמִי יָחוּשׁ חוּץ מִמֶּנִּי.

For who will eat, who will hasten to satisfy my craving, but me? (Kohelet 2:25)

At this stage in the Garden, Adam is the only one who eats.

וַיִּקְרָא הָאָדָם שֵׁמוֹת לְכָל־הַבְּהֵמָה וּלְעוֹף הַשָּׁמַיִם וּלְכֹל חַיַּת הַשָּׂדֶה וּלְאָדָם לֹא־מָצָא עֵזֶר כְּנֶגְדּוֹ. So the **man** gave **names** to all the animals, the birds of the heavens, and all the wild creatures. But **Adam found no** fitting helper for himself. (Bereshit 2:20)	מַה־שֶּׁהָיָה כְּבָר נִקְרָא שְׁמוֹ וְנוֹדָע אֲשֶׁר־הוּא אָדָם וְלֹא־יוּכַל לָדִין עִם שֶׁתַּקִּיף מִמֶּנּוּ. Whatever has been was already **named** – and it is known that this is but a **man** [*adam*], who cannot contend with one more powerful than he. (Kohelet 6:10)
	אֲשֶׁר עוֹד־בִּקְשָׁה נַפְשִׁי וְלֹא מָצָאתִי אָדָם אֶחָד מֵאֶלֶף מָצָאתִי וְאִשָּׁה בְכָל־אֵלֶּה לֹא מָצָאתִי. This too my soul sought and **did not find**: one **man** [*adam*] in a thousand I found, but among those even one woman I **did not find.** (Kohelet 7:28)

The two verses in Kohelet refer to how Adam first gave names to the animals[4] ("gave names," "was named"), but among the animals did not find a "fitting helper," "a woman," for a mate.[5]

---

3. Clemens, "The Law of Sin and Death," 7, notes that in Kohelet, as in Bereshit, "greed is a correlate of pride, and unfulfillment is its consequence." Kohelet reviews greed in 4:4–8, 5:10–17, and 6:1–9.

4. Targum on Kohelet 6:10 says the verse refers to Adam. See also Ralbag on Kohelet 6:10.

5. While Kohelet 7:28 discusses finding a man, the strong linguistic parallels to Bereshit 2:20 hint to Adam's search for a mate. Ibn Ezra on Kohelet 7:29 says the above verse

NAKEDNESS

וַיִּהְיוּ שְׁנֵיהֶם **עֲרוּמִים** הָאָדָם וְאִשְׁתּוֹ וְלֹא יִתְבֹּשָׁשׁוּ.	כַּאֲשֶׁר יָצָא מִבֶּטֶן אִמּוֹ **עָרוֹם** יָשׁוּב לָלֶכֶת כְּשֶׁבָּא וּמְאוּמָה לֹא־יִשָּׂא בַעֲמָלוֹ שֶׁיֹּלֵךְ בְּיָדוֹ.
The man and his wife were both **naked** [*arumim*], but they were not ashamed. (Bereshit 2:25)	**Naked** [*arom*] as he emerged from his mother's womb, so will he return. And not the slightest thing from all his labor will he retain to take with him. (Kohelet 5:14)

The verse in Kohelet reflects how Adam was naked when he was created, and how he lived that way in the Garden. Adam's nakedness will have more significance as the story progresses.

SNAKES

וְהַנָּחָשׁ הָיָה **עָרוּם** מִכֹּל חַיַּת הַשָּׂדֶה אֲשֶׁר עָשָׂה יְהוָה אֱלֹהִים וַיֹּאמֶר אֶל־הָאִשָּׁה אַף כִּי־אָמַר אֱלֹהִים לֹא תֹאכְלוּ מִכֹּל עֵץ הַגָּן.	חֹפֵר גּוּמָץ בּוֹ יִפּוֹל וּפֹרֵץ גָּדֵר יִשְּׁכֶנּוּ נָחָשׁ. He who digs a pit may fall into it, and he who breaches a fence – a **snake** may bite him. (Kohelet 10:8)
The **snake** was the **shrewd-est** [*arum*] of all the wild animals the Lord God had made. "Did God say," it asked the woman, "that you must not eat from any tree in the Garden?" (Bereshit 3:1)	אִם־יִשֹּׁךְ הַנָּחָשׁ בְּלוֹא־לָחַשׁ וְאֵין יִתְרוֹן לְבַעַל הַלָּשׁוֹן. If the **snake** bites without utterance [by the charmer], there is no profit to the charmer [lit., "master of the tongue"]. (Kohelet 10:11)

The above two verses in Kohelet both mention a snake and are parallel to the introduction of the snake in the Eden story. In

---

(7:28) indicates that one woman should be enough for a man (like the one wife for Adam), as compared with Shlomo, who had 1,000 wives.

Bereshit, the snake is noted for being shrewd; Kohelet warns us about snakes. In the first Kohelet verse, the narrator mentions "breaching a fence." This is precisely what the snake encouraged the woman to do – to breach the fence God had placed around the Tree of Knowledge.[6] In the second Kohelet verse, we see that if the victim does not use the power of speech ["mastery of the tongue"] against the perpetrator, damage will ensue. Likewise, the woman did not use her power of speech to argue against the lies of the snake, and great damage was done.

6. The Sages interpreted Kohelet 10:8 as a "fence of law." See *Tosefta* Hullin 2:6; Avoda Zara 27b.

Chapter 5

Adam – The Punishment

THE DEBACLE AND ITS FALLOUT

וַיֹּאמֶר הָאָדָם **הָאִשָּׁה אֲשֶׁר נָתַתָּה** עִמָּדִי הִוא נָתְנָה־לִּי מִן־הָעֵץ וָאֹכֵל.

The man said, "**The woman that You gave** to be with me – she gave me from the tree, and I ate." (Bereshit 3:12)

רְאֵה חַיִּים עִם־**אִשָּׁה אֲשֶׁר־אָהַבְתָּ** כָּל־יְמֵי חַיֵּי הֶבְלֶךָ **אֲשֶׁר נָתַן**־לְךָ תַּחַת הַשֶּׁמֶשׁ כֹּל יְמֵי הֶבְלֶךָ כִּי הוּא חֶלְקְךָ בַּחַיִּים וּבַעֲמָלְךָ אֲשֶׁר־אַתָּה עָמֵל תַּחַת הַשָּׁמֶשׁ.

Enjoy life with the **woman** you love all the days of fleeting breath, that He **has given** you here beneath the sun, for this is your share in life, your due for all your toil, all your labor beneath the sun. (Kohelet 9:9)

וּמוֹצֶא אֲנִי מַר מִמָּוֶת אֶת־**הָאִשָּׁה אֲשֶׁר־הִיא** מְצוֹדִים...

And this is what I found: **woman** is more bitter than death, for she is all traps... (Kohelet 7:26)

49

These verses all describe a woman (followed by the preposition *asher* – "that"). In Kohelet 9:9, we also see the verb "give," which matches the same verb found in the verse from Bereshit.[1]

In Kohelet 7:26, the woman is criticized for her role in the tree story – connecting her with death. However, in 9:9, she is referred to in a positive way, mentioning life. This indicates a complicated relationship; Adam loved her, but also blamed her for what happened, and that must have continued even after the expulsion from the Garden.

וּלְאָדָם אָמַר כִּי־שָׁמַעְתָּ לְקוֹל אִשְׁתֶּךָ וַתֹּאכַל מִן־הָעֵץ אֲשֶׁר צִוִּיתִיךָ לֵאמֹר לֹא תֹאכַל מִמֶּנּוּ אֲרוּרָה הָאֲדָמָה בַּעֲבוּרֶךָ **בְּעִצָּבוֹן** תֹּאכְלֶנָּה **כֹּל יְמֵי חַיֶּיךָ**.	כִּי בְּרֹב חָכְמָה רָב־כָּעַס וְיוֹסִיף דַּעַת יוֹסִיף מַכְאוֹב.
To **Adam** He said, "Because you **listened** to the voice of your wife and ate of the tree from which I commanded you not to eat – cursed will be the land on your account. With **anguish** you will eat from it **all the days** of your life." (Bereshit 3:17)	For in great wisdom lies great bitterness; and one who gathers knowledge gathers pain. (Kohelet 1:18)
	גַּם לְכָל־הַדְּבָרִים אֲשֶׁר יְדַבֵּרוּ אַל־תִּתֵּן לִבֶּךָ אֲשֶׁר לֹא־**תִשְׁמַע** אֶת־עַבְדְּךָ מְקַלְלֶךָ.
	Also, do not pay attention to everything that is said; do not **listen to** your slave when he curses you. (Kohelet 7:21)
	כִּי מֶה־הֹוֶה **לָאָדָם** בְּכָל־עֲמָלוֹ וּבְרַעְיוֹן לִבּוֹ שֶׁהוּא עָמֵל תַּחַת הַשָּׁמֶשׁ: כִּי **כָל־יָמָיו** מַכְאֹבִים וָכַעַס עִנְיָנוֹ גַּם־בַּלַּיְלָה לֹא־שָׁכַב לִבּוֹ גַּם־זֶה הֶבֶל הוּא.
	For what does a **man** have for all the labor and of all the thought that he has expended under the sun? **All his days** are pain, his occupation bitterness, and even at night his mind does not rest – and this too is futile. (Kohelet 2:22–23)

---

1. It is not clear what is being given in Kohelet 9:9. While most translations indicate it is the "fleeting days," Zer-Kavod in *Daat Mikra* conjectures that it is the woman (and makes a comparison between our verse and Bereshit).

מַסִּיעַ אֲבָנִים **יֵעָצֵב** בָּהֶם בּוֹקֵעַ עֵצִים יִסָּכֶן בָּם.

He who quarries stones will be **hurt** by them; he who chops trees will be harmed by them. (Kohelet 10:9)

The verse in Bereshit describes the curse Adam received for listening to his wife (instead of listening to God's command). Adam could have easily eaten from all the other trees but ate from the forbidden Tree of Knowledge. As a punishment, he would be able to eat only after arduous work.

The parallel verses in Kohelet all reflect this. In 1:18, Adam realizes that by "gathering knowledge," i.e., eating from the Tree of Knowledge, he added pain and heartache to his life. Kohelet 7:21 warns against listening to "everything that is said." This is precisely what angers God – "because you listened" (Bereshit 3:17). Adam's wife should not have listened to the snake, and Adam should not have listened to his wife. They should have listened to God. Now, as punishment, they must listen to the curse.[2] In Kohelet 2:22–23, Adam recognizes that because of the curse, he will toil in pain and anguish "all his days."[3]

Kohelet 10:9, describing the dangers of physical labor, has two parts, each reflecting Adam's sin and punishment. The first part says "will be hurt," using the verb *ye'atzev*, which is parallel to the *be'itzavon* – "with anguish" found in the verse from Bereshit. The second part mentions the cutting or splitting of trees. When Ḥava took the fruit from the Tree of Knowledge, she tore the fruit from its branch on the tree.

---

2. God clearly is not "your slave" in 7:21, but we will see below why Kohelet mentions it in this context.
3. Regarding "all the days" in Bereshit and "all his days" in Kohelet, Moxham notes ("Qohelet's Fall," 104), "This is a comparatively rare expression…this shared language gives further evidence of the connection" between Bereshit 3 and Kohelet.

וְקוֹץ וְדַרְדַּר תַּצְמִיחַ לָךְ וְאָכַלְתָּ אֶת־עֵשֶׂב הַשָּׂדֶה.	מַה־יִּתְרוֹן לָאָדָם בְּכָל־עֲמָלוֹ שֶׁיַּעֲמֹל תַּחַת הַשָּׁמֶשׁ.
It will sprout thorns and thistles for you, and you shall eat grass of the field. (Bereshit 3:18)	What profit remains for all the labor one toils beneath the sun? (Kohelet 1:3)
	וּפָנִיתִי אֲנִי בְּכָל־מַעֲשַׂי שֶׁעָשׂוּ יָדַי וּבֶעָמָל שֶׁעָמַלְתִּי לַעֲשׂוֹת וְהִנֵּה הַכֹּל הֶבֶל וּרְעוּת רוּחַ וְאֵין יִתְרוֹן תַּחַת הַשָּׁמֶשׁ.
	And then I turned to look at all my works, at the work of my hands, at all that I had labored to achieve – and this is what I saw: it was all futile, nothing but pursuit of wind, and there is no true profit beneath the sun. (Kohelet 2:11)
	בַּבֹּקֶר זְרַע אֶת־זַרְעֶךָ וְלָעֶרֶב אַל־תַּנַּח יָדֶךָ כִּי אֵינְךָ יוֹדֵעַ אֵי זֶה יִכְשָׁר הֲזֶה אוֹ־זֶה וְאִם־שְׁנֵיהֶם כְּאֶחָד טוֹבִים.
	Sow your seeds in the morning, and come evening do not lay your hands to rest – for you do not know which will succeed, these seeds or those, or whether the two are as good as one another. (Kohelet 11:6)

In Bereshit 3:18, God curses Adam with a life of hard work, and Adam learns his hard work will be for naught; instead of harvesting produce, he will grow thorns and thistles. The verses in Kohelet highlight Adam's frustrations with this new reality. What is the point of all that work?

This stands in contrast to Bereshit 2:5, which describes the state before the creation of man: "No shrub of the field yet grew on earth, and no plant had yet sprouted, for the Lord God had not yet brought rain upon the earth, and there was no man to work the land." The plants couldn't grow without man's help. Kohelet 11:6 notes that now, even when man works in the field, he does not know if he will succeed:[4] "The land has the advantage over all; even a king is enslaved to the field" (Kohelet 5:8).

When Adam lived in the Garden, he was responsible for the land, but was its master. After the expulsion, he had to work for his food. He became a servant to the field, hoping for rations, which did not always come.

THE INTRODUCTION OF DEATH INTO THE WORLD

וּמֵעֵץ הַדַּעַת טוֹב וָרָע לֹא תֹאכַל מִמֶּנּוּ כִּי בְּיוֹם אֲכָלְךָ מִמֶּנּוּ **מוֹת תָּמוּת**.	כִּי מִקְרֶה בְנֵי־הָאָדָם וּמִקְרֶה הַבְּהֵמָה וּמִקְרֶה אֶחָד לָהֶם כְּמוֹת זֶה כֵּן **מוֹת** זֶה וְרוּחַ אֶחָד לַכֹּל וּמוֹתַר הָאָדָם מִן־הַבְּהֵמָה אָיִן כִּי הַכֹּל הָבֶל.
But the Tree of Knowledge of good and bad – you may not eat from that, for on the day you eat from it, you will **surely die** [*mot tamut*]. (Bereshit 2:17)	For the fate of man is the fate of cattle: the same fate awaits them both, the **death** of one is like the **death** of the other, their life-breath is the same, and the preeminence of man over beast is nothing, for it is all futile. (Kohelet 3:19)

One of the consequences of eating from the tree was the introduction of death into the world. In Kohelet, Adam feels that

---

4. Kohelet 11:1–6 is dedicated to advice to (or from) farmers. This seems out of place in a work composed by a king, but very much fits Adam's new life, where he must succeed at agriculture. In these six verses, a phrase meaning "you do not know" or "you will not know" appears four times. For Adam, this is ironic. When he was in the Garden, he did not need to perform all the agricultural tasks described there. But then he ate from the Tree of Knowledge, and yet did not gain knowledge. In fact, now he does not even know where his food will come from.

since both humans and animals die, there is no difference between them. Adam earlier believed he was unique, for when he was created, God "breathed the breath of life into his nostrils" (Bereshit 2:7). Now he realizes they both have the "same life-breath." This can help explain the previous verse, which is difficult to understand:

אָמַרְתִּי אֲנִי בְּלִבִּי עַל־דִּבְרַת בְּנֵי הָאָדָם לְבָרָם הָאֱלֹהִים וְלִרְאוֹת שְׁהֶם־בְּהֵמָה הֵמָּה לָהֶם.

I would translate it as follows: "I said in my heart concerning humans that God has chosen them, but I have seen that they themselves are as animals" (Kohelet 3:18). At first, Adam thought humans were different from the beasts because God distinguished them, but he then learned that they both suffer the same fate.

בְּזֵעַת אַפֶּיךָ תֹּאכַל לֶחֶם עַד שׁוּבְךָ אֶל־הָאֲדָמָה כִּי מִמֶּנָּה לֻקָּחְתָּ **כִּי־עָפָר אַתָּה וְאֶל־עָפָר תָּשׁוּב.** By the sweat of your brow will you eat bread until you return to the land, for from there you were taken. **You are dust, and you will return to dust**. (Bereshit 3:19)	הַכֹּל הוֹלֵךְ אֶל־מָקוֹם אֶחָד **הַכֹּל הָיָה** מִן־הֶעָפָר וְהַכֹּל שָׁב אֶל־הֶעָפָר. All end up in the same place; **all come from dust, and all return to dust.** (Kohelet 3:20)
	וְיָשֹׁב הֶעָפָר עַל־הָאָרֶץ כְּשֶׁהָיָה וְהָרוּחַ תָּשׁוּב אֶל־הָאֱלֹהִים אֲשֶׁר נְתָנָהּ. **The dust returns** to the earth where it began, and the life-breath returns to God who gave it. (Kohelet 12:7)

At the end of God's curse of man, He concludes with the poetic phrase "you are dust, and you will return to dust."[5] In Kohelet 3:20,

---

5. Moxham ("Qohelet's Fall," 63) points out that in Bereshit, only Adam is formed from dust and returns to dust. Kohelet, echoing Adam, returns to the idea that everyone

we find an almost exact replica of the phrase.[6] Later, in 12:7, there is another reference to the return to dust, together with mention of Adam's creation by means of God's life-breath.

ADAM'S KOHELET-SPECIFIC INSIGHTS

Finally, there are verses in Kohelet without linguistic parallels in Bereshit, but which reflect Adam's feelings after hearing the curse. Here he recalls rationalizing his behavior: "Do not let your mouth lead your flesh to sin, and do not tell the messenger that it was a mistake; why should you have God rage at your words and destroy the work of your hands?" (Kohelet 5:5).

He later recognizes the folly of that approach: "Yes, all that I found is this: that God made man upright; but they have sought out many schemes" (7:29).

God created man to be righteous,[7] but it was Adam who sinned. Had he taken responsibility for it and not blamed others, God would not have been as angry with him and would not have sabotaged his efforts in working the land.

He then acknowledges that what God has done – the punishment, particularly that of death – cannot be undone: "Consider the acts of God – for nobody can straighten what He[8] has twisted [*ivto*]?" (7:13).

Kohelet goes on to make a general statement about the flawed nature of humanity. But as we see in many verses of the book, the word *adam* can also suggest the specific person of Adam, and not

---

is from dust, and applies that verse to all humanity.

6. One difference, as pointed out by the *Metzudat David* commentary, is that Kohelet is saying both humans and animals originate in dust and return to dust in death.

7. Rashi on this verse suggests this interpretation. He also points out that the verse starts out in the singular ("man") but then continues in the plural ("they"), indicating the creation of woman from man. See also Ramban on Bereshit 2:9, who discusses this verse in Kohelet in the context of Adam in the Garden.

8. Rashi and Ibn Ezra, presumably disinclined to attribute the negative connotations to God on this verse, say man is the one who has twisted. However, in Iyov 19:6, we find the same verb used to describe God's actions (*ivtani*).

only the general collective of humankind. Read that way, in this verse, Adam admits he has sinned, and has not done good:

כִּי אָדָם אֵין צַדִּיק בָּאָרֶץ אֲשֶׁר יַעֲשֶׂה־טּוֹב וְלֹא יֶחֱטָא.

> For there is not a righteous man [*adam*] on earth who does good and doesn't sin. (7:20)

Even though we never read of Adam recognizing his sin, Kohelet does include that acknowledgment, which is the first step to eventual repentance.

Chapter 6

Kayin and Hevel

T he following two verses, one occurring at the beginning of Kohelet, the other in the last chapter, serve as bookends to the narrative:

הֲבֵל הֲבָלִים אָמַר קֹהֶלֶת הֲבֵל הֲבָלִים הַכֹּל הָבֶל.

Utter **futility** [*havel havelim*], Kohelet said. Utter **futility** – it is all **futile**. (Kohelet 1:2)

דִּבְרֵי חֲכָמִים כַּדָּרְבֹנוֹת וּכְמַשְׂמְרוֹת נְטוּעִים בַּעֲלֵי אֲסֻפּוֹת נִתְּנוּ מֵרֹעֶה אֶחָד.

The words of the wise are like goads; like pointed nails are the scholars' sayings. One **shepherd** gave them all. (12:11)

The word *hevel* appears thirty-eight times in the book of Kohelet.[1]
It literally means "breath" or "vapor," and is generally translated
as "futility" or "vanity."[2] Of course, it is also the name of Adam's
son Hevel, who was the first human to die.

The repetition of the word *hevel* in this opening verse (and
throughout the book) reflects Adam bemoaning his dead son,
Hevel. It is noteworthy that Hevel tried to break free of the curse
of labor by becoming a shepherd (*ro'eh*), and not working the land
like his brother Kayin:

וַתֹּסֶף לָלֶדֶת אֶת־אָחִיו אֶת־**הָבֶל** וַיְהִי־**הֶבֶל רֹעֵה צֹאן** וְקַיִן הָיָה עֹבֵד
אֲדָמָה.

She then gave birth to his brother **Hevel**. **Hevel** became a
shepherd, while Kayin was a worker of the land. (Bereshit
4:2)

In the end, however, Hevel's life was cut short. It was futile (*hevel*)
to have tried.[3]

In Kohelet 12:11, Adam says he learned his lessons from a shepherd – his son Hevel. However, Hevel did not teach him via sayings and proverbs, but through the goads of painful experience.

---

1. And only thirty-five times in the rest of the Tanakh.
2. Vanity in the sense of worthlessness, not pride.
3. Note that the Hebrew word for shepherd, *ro'eh* (רֹעֶה), has the same root as the
   word *re'ut* (רעות). Fox (*The JPS Bible Commentary: Ecclesiastes*, p. xx) notes that in
   Kohelet, the phrase *re'ut ruah* "is almost always paired with *hevel* and also implies
   senselessness." He translates the term as "pursuit of wind." However, he continues, it
   is "an ambiguous expression," since *re'ut* has a number of possible meanings, one of
   which is "shepherd" (as suggested by Seforno on Kohelet 1:14). "Shepherd of wind"
   (or breath) is an apt description of Hevel, which explains the pairing of *re'ut* with
   hevel. See also Hoshea 12:2, which describes Efrayim as *ro'eh ruah*.

וַיְהִי מִקֵּץ יָמִים וַיָּבֵא קַיִן מִפְּרִי הָאֲדָמָה מִנְחָה לַיהוָה. וְהֶבֶל הֵבִיא גַם־הוּא מִבְּכֹרוֹת צֹאנוֹ וּמֵחֶלְבֵהֶן וַיִּשַׁע יְהוָה אֶל־הֶבֶל וְאֶל־מִנְחָתוֹ.	הַכֹּל כַּאֲשֶׁר לַכֹּל מִקְרֶה אֶחָד לַצַּדִּיק וְלָרָשָׁע לַטּוֹב וְלַטָּהוֹר וְלַטָּמֵא וְלַזֹּבֵחַ וְלַאֲשֶׁר אֵינֶנּוּ זֹבֵחַ כַּטּוֹב כַּחֹטֶא הַנִּשְׁבָּע כַּאֲשֶׁר שְׁבוּעָה יָרֵא.
Time passed, and Kayin brought fruit of the land as an offering to the Lord. Hevel too brought an offering: the best portions from the firstborn of his flock. The Lord looked favorably on Hevel and his offering. (Bereshit 4:3–4)	All is as it is for all. The same fate awaits the righteous and the wicked; the good and the pure and the impure; the one who sacrifices and the one who does not sacrifice; for a good man just as for a sinner; and for the one who swears along with the one who shuns oaths. (Kohelet 9:2)

In the Bereshit verses, we continue to see the differences between Kayin and Hevel. The Kohelet verse, too, provides a dichotomy between different types of people; on the one hand the righteous and pure, on the other hand wicked and impure – and still, they both have the same fate. They all will die.

Kohelet also writes of "the one who sacrifices and the one who does not sacrifice." A reading of the story of Kayin and Hevel gives rise to the question, "Didn't both brothers bring sacrifices?" However, a closer examination of the Hebrew word for sacrifice, *zove'ah*, will show that it applies only to the sacrifice of animals. Therefore, Hevel was *zove'ah* and Kayin was not *zove'ah*. Hevel was righteous and pure (purity in the Tanakh is also closely associated with sacrifices and the Temple), and Kayin was wicked, and, due to his contact with Hevel's dead body, impure.[4] One might assume

---

4. The verse also mentions one "who swears" and one "who shuns oaths." There is no mention of oaths in the story of Kayin and Hevel. However, the book of Kohelet repeatedly warns for caution regarding oaths and vows (e.g., 5:1–6). Moxham ("Qohelet's Fall," 154) relates these verses to the Bereshit story: "[Hevel] is slow to sacrifice" (not being the first to do so), "while [Kayin] is precipitous." He also notes

that Hevel's righteousness and purity, not to mention his (pleasing) sacrifices, would protect him, yet they did not.

וְאֶל־קַיִן וְאֶל־מִנְחָתוֹ לֹא שָׁעָה וַיִּחַר לְקַיִן מְאֹד וַיִּפְּלוּ פָּנָיו.	וְרָאִיתִי אֲנִי אֶת־כָּל־עָמָל וְאֵת כָּל־כִּשְׁרוֹן הַמַּעֲשֶׂה כִּי הִיא קִנְאַת־אִישׁ מֵרֵעֵהוּ גַּם־זֶה הֶבֶל וּרְעוּת רוּחַ.
But upon Kayin and his offering He did not look with favor. Kayin became very angry, and his face fell. (Bereshit 4:5)	And I saw that all the striving and all the skill: it is all but one man's jealousy of another. This too is futile and pursuit of wind. (Kohelet 4:4)

Kayin was jealous of Hevel; and the Hebrew word for jealousy, *kin'a*, recalls the name Kayin. It is noteworthy that the Kohelet verse above uses the far less frequent term for man in Kohelet: *ish* instead of *adam*. This recalls what his mother said as she named him: *kaniti ish*, "I have made a man" (Bereshit 4:1).

Kohelet, as Adam, bemoans his loss:

> There is one who is alone, with no fellow, no son, nor brother. And there is no end to all his labor, nor will his eye be sated with riches: "For whom, after all, am I laboring and denying myself goodness?" This too is futility and a wretched business. (Kohelet 4:8)

Adam has no brother, and now neither does he have his son Hevel. No matter how much he works, he is never satisfied – neither

---

there is no mention of Hevel speaking at all, which fits Kohelet's charge, "Let your words be few" (5:1). Perhaps Kohelet is hinting to another subplot, where Kayin vowed to bring one kind of sacrifice but never fulfilled that vow. That could be his "sin" (Bereshit 4:7) and the reason his sacrifice was rejected. See parallel verses in Devarim 23:22–24, where we are told that anyone not fulfilling his vow to God "will have committed a sin" (23:22).

materially or emotionally. It would have been better had both brothers remained alive and worked together, instead of just one surviving: "Two are better than one, for they have greater benefit from their labor" (4:9).

וְאֶל־קַיִן וְאֶל־מִנְחָתוֹ לֹא שָׁעָה וַיִּחַר לְקַיִן מְאֹד **וַיִּפְּלוּ** פָּנָיו. וַיֹּאמֶר יְהוָה אֶל־קַיִן לָמָּה חָרָה לָךְ וְלָמָּה **נָפְלוּ** פָנֶיךָ. הֲלוֹא אִם־תֵּיטִיב שְׂאֵת וְאִם לֹא תֵיטִיב לַפֶּתַח חַטָּאת רֹבֵץ וְאֵלֶיךָ תְּשׁוּקָתוֹ וְאַתָּה תִּמְשָׁל־בּוֹ. וַיֹּאמֶר קַיִן אֶל־הֶבֶל אָחִיו וַיְהִי בִּהְיוֹתָם בַּשָּׂדֶה **וַיָּקָם** קַיִן אֶל־הֶבֶל אָחִיו וַיַּהַרְגֵהוּ.	כִּי אִם־**יִפֹּלוּ** הָאֶחָד **יָקִים** אֶת־חֲבֵרוֹ וְאִילוֹ הָאֶחָד **שֶׁיִּפּוֹל** וְאֵין שֵׁנִי **לַהֲקִימוֹ**.
	For if one **falls** down, the other will **raise** him; but pity the one who **falls** alone, with no one to **raise** him. (Kohelet 4:10)
But upon Kayin and his offering He did not look with favor. Kayin became very angry, and his face **fell**. The Lord said to Kayin: "Why are you angry; why is your face **fallen**?" … Kayin talked to his brother Hevel, and when they were in the field, Kayin **rose** up against his brother Hevel and killed him. (Bereshit 4:5–8)	
כִּי שִׁבְעָתַיִם **יֻקַּם**־קָיִן וְלֶמֶךְ שִׁבְעִים וְשִׁבְעָה.	
If Kayin will be **avenged** [lit., risen up] seven times, then Lemekh seventy-seven. (Bereshit 4:24)	

In the story of Kayin and Hevel, the verbs "raise" and "fall" appear repeatedly. Kohelet 4:10 uses them multiple times as well. But unlike in this verse, where when one falls the other helps him up, in Bereshit, Kayin rises up to kill Hevel.

Hevel came into the world, but departed into the darkness of the earth, and even his name is covered up there:

כִּי־בַהֶבֶל בָּא וּבַחֹשֶׁךְ יֵלֵךְ וּבַחֹשֶׁךְ שְׁמוֹ יְכֻסֶּה:

For he comes in futility [*hevel*] and leaves in darkness, and
in darkness is his name covered over. (Kohelet 6:4)

Adam mourns Hevel. He begins to grasp the permanency of death,
which had been unfamiliar to him previously. Kayin, the live dog,
is better off than Hevel, the dead lion:

כִּי־מִי אֲשֶׁר יְחֻבַּר אֶל כָּל־הַחַיִּים יֵשׁ בִּטָּחוֹן כִּי־לְכֶלֶב חַי הוּא טוֹב
מִן־הָאַרְיֵה הַמֵּת. כִּי הַחַיִּים יוֹדְעִים שֶׁיָּמֻתוּ וְהַמֵּתִים אֵינָם יוֹדְעִים
מְאוּמָה וְאֵין־עוֹד לָהֶם שָׂכָר כִּי נִשְׁכַּח זִכְרָם.

For anyone still bound to life has something to rely upon:
"Better to be a living dog than a dead lion." For the living
know at least that they must die, while the dead know nothing. No longer rewarded for their actions, their memories
are forgotten. (Kohelet 9:4–5)

וַיֵּדַע אָדָם עוֹד אֶת־אִשְׁתּוֹ וַתֵּלֶד בֵּן וַתִּקְרָא אֶת־שְׁמוֹ שֵׁת כִּי שָׁת־לִי אֱלֹהִים זֶרַע אַחֵר תַּחַת הֶבֶל כִּי הֲרָגוֹ קָיִן.	רָאִיתִי אֶת־כָּל־הַחַיִּים הַמְהַלְּכִים תַּחַת הַשֶּׁמֶשׁ עִם הַיֶּלֶד הַשֵּׁנִי אֲשֶׁר יַעֲמֹד תַּחְתָּיו.
Adam knew his wife again, and she gave birth to a son and named him Shet (Seth), "because God has granted me another child **instead** of Hevel," for Kayin had killed him. (Bereshit 4:25)	Yes, I saw all of life moving about under the sun, with the next child who will stand **in his stead**. (Kohelet 4:15)

In these verses, Adam is referring to his third son, Shet, who
"replaced" Hevel.

אֶת־הַכֹּל רָאִיתִי בִּימֵי הֶבְלִי יֵשׁ צַדִּיק אֹבֵד בְּצִדְקוֹ וְיֵשׁ רָשָׁע מַאֲרִיךְ
בְּרָעָתוֹ.

I have seen it all in the days of my futility: righteous men
who die in spite of their righteousness, and wicked ones
who live long in spite of their wickedness. (Kohelet 7:15)

The phrase "in the days of my futility" can be read as "in the days of
my *Hevel*." Adam learned, in the days of *his* Hevel, that sometimes
the righteous perish and the wicked endure.[5] Hevel died before
his time; and although Kayin was punished, he did continue to
live a long life.[6]

It is also possible that Adam viewed himself as the wicked
one who should have been punished with the first death (since
he ate from the tree) instead of Hevel, but instead Adam lived
a long life. He bemoans delayed punishment (for himself or for
Kayin) in Kohelet: "Because judgment against an evil act is not
executed speedily, people's hearts fill up with thoughts of doing
evil. A sinner does a hundred evil deeds and is granted long years
for it" (Kohelet 8:11–12).

He then continues to describe a situation where there seems
to be no justice at all:

יֶשׁ־הֶבֶל אֲשֶׁר נַעֲשָׂה עַל־הָאָרֶץ אֲשֶׁר יֵשׁ צַדִּיקִים אֲשֶׁר מַגִּיעַ אֲלֵהֶם
כְּמַעֲשֵׂה הָרְשָׁעִים וְיֵשׁ רְשָׁעִים שֶׁמַּגִּיעַ אֲלֵהֶם כְּמַעֲשֵׂה הַצַּדִּיקִים
אָמַרְתִּי שֶׁגַּם־זֶה הָבֶל.

---

5. Although the translation here says that the righteous perish despite their righteousness and the wicked endure despite their wickedness, it could be argued that, at least
   in the case of Kayin and Hevel, the righteous man perished *because* of his righteousness – Hevel's "righteousness" was the reason Kayin killed him. And Kayin endured,
   because of his wickedness – he no longer had any competition.
6. Certainly, Kayin lived longer than Hevel, and Rashi's understanding of Bereshit 4:23
   indicates that he lived for another five generations.

Yet see this thing of futility [*hevel*] that happens on this earth:
the righteous who suffer the same fate as the wicked; and
the wicked who enjoy the same fate as the righteous – and
I say: this too is futile. (8:14)[7]

As said in Kohelet 7:15, Adam is frustrated when the righteous suffer and the wicked prosper.

---

7. Another example of this is Kohelet 6:1–2:

> There is an evil I have seen beneath the sun, and the harm it does people is
> great. There will be a man to whom God gives wealth, possessions, and honor
> so that he lacks nothing his heart desires. And then God will not grant him the
> power to partake of it, and a stranger will consume it all; this is futility [*hevel*]
> and an evil sickness.

Hevel did not get the opportunity to enjoy his bounty. These verses indicate that
perhaps Kayin availed himself of Hevel's property.

Chapter 7

The End of Adam's Life

זֶה סֵפֶר תּוֹלְדֹת אָדָם בְּיוֹם בְּרֹא אֱלֹהִים אָדָם בִּדְמוּת אֱלֹהִים עָשָׂה אֹתוֹ.	דּוֹר הֹלֵךְ וְדוֹר בָּא וְהָאָרֶץ לְעוֹלָם עֹמָדֶת.
This is the book of Adam's generations. On the day that God created man, He made him in the likeness of God. (Bereshit 5:1)	One generation leaves, another comes; but the earth remains forever. (Kohelet 1:4)

At the end of his long life, Adam reviews the generations that followed him.

וַיִּהְיוּ יְמֵי־אָדָם אַחֲרֵי הוֹלִידוֹ אֶת־שֵׁת שְׁמֹנֶה מֵאֹת שָׁנָה וַיּוֹלֶד בָּנִים וּבָנוֹת. וַיִּהְיוּ כָּל־יְמֵי אָדָם אֲשֶׁר־חַי תְּשַׁע מֵאוֹת שָׁנָה וּשְׁלֹשִׁים שָׁנָה וַיָּמֹת.	אִם־יוֹלִיד אִישׁ מֵאָה וְשָׁנִים רַבּוֹת יִחְיֶה וְרַב שֶׁיִּהְיוּ יְמֵי־שָׁנָיו וְנַפְשׁוֹ לֹא־תִשְׂבַּע מִן־הַטּוֹבָה וְגַם־קְבוּרָה לֹא־הָיְתָה לּוֹ אָמַרְתִּי טוֹב מִמֶּנּוּ הַנָּפֶל.
After Shet was born, Adam lived eight hundred years and had other sons and daughters. Altogether Adam lived nine hundred and thirty years, and then he died. (Bereshit 5:4–5)	A man may have a hundred children and live for many years, and as many as his years may be, if he is never satisfied with all that goodness – I say a stillborn [lit., fallen one] – lacking a burial,[1] is better off than he. (Kohelet 6:3)
	וְאִלּוּ חָיָה אֶלֶף שָׁנִים פַּעֲמַיִם וְטוֹבָה לֹא רָאָה הֲלֹא אֶל־מָקוֹם אֶחָד הַכֹּל הוֹלֵךְ.
	Even if he lived a thousand years twice over, he saw no good. Well, do we not all go to the same place in the end? (Kohelet 6:6)

Adam lived a long life, nearly a thousand years, and had hundreds of descendants in his lifetime. But "he was never satisfied with that goodness" and "he saw no good." Why? Because his son Hevel was better than he was. He refers to Hevel as a stillborn (literally, "the fallen one"), since his short life made it seem as if he had never been born at all; and he did not even receive a proper burial.[2]

---

1. This verse is difficult to interpret. I prefer the interpretation that identifies the stillborn as the one without a burial, as opposed to the man described in the verse. The stillborn did not receive burials, and this also fits the next verse (6:4), which describes one whose very name is covered in darkness.
2. The Midrash (*Shemot Rabba* 31:17) identifies Hevel as the "fallen one" in this verse.

כִּי מִי־יוֹדֵעַ מַה־טּוֹב לָאָדָם בַּחַיִּים מִסְפַּר יְמֵי־חַיֵּי הֶבְלוֹ **וְיַעֲשֵׂם כַּצֵּל** אֲשֶׁר מִי־יַגִּיד לָאָדָם מַה־יִּהְיֶה אַחֲרָיו תַּחַת הַשָּׁמֶשׁ.

For who knows what is good **for a man** [*adam*] in life, during the numbered days of his futility, which he **makes as a shadow**; for who can tell man [*adam*] what his fate will be under the sun? (Kohelet 6:12)

After everything he has been through, Adam rhetorically asks, "Who knows what is good for *adam* in life?" He now understands that only God knows what is good, and it was wrong of him to think he could determine this on his own. He follows up by asking, "Who can tell *adam* what his fate will be?" Again, the answer is clearly God. Why? Because God created him. This is alluded to in the phrase "makes as a shadow." The Hebrew, *veya'asem katzel*, has a parallel in Bereshit, where after the Flood, God explicitly prohibits murder:

שֹׁפֵךְ דַּם הָאָדָם בָּאָדָם דָּמוֹ יִשָּׁפֵךְ כִּי **בְּצֶלֶם** אֱלֹהִים **עָשָׂה** אֶת־הָאָדָם.

One who sheds the blood of man – by man shall his blood be shed, for in God's image **man** was **made**. (Bereshit 9:6)

The word for image, *tzelem*, is similar to the word for shadow, *tzel*.[3] The linguistic parallels therefore support the idea that because God created man in His image (shadow), man should therefore trust God to know what is good, and what will happen in the future.

---

3. See Abrabanel on Bereshit 1:26.

וַיְצַו יְהוָה אֱלֹהִים עַל־הָאָדָם לֵאמֹר
מִכֹּל עֵץ־הַגָּן אָכֹל תֹּאכֵל. וּמֵעֵץ
הַדַּעַת **טוֹב וָרָע** לֹא תֹאכַל מִמֶּנּוּ כִּי
בְּיוֹם אֲכָלְךָ מִמֶּנּוּ מוֹת תָּמוּת.

And the Lord **God commanded**
the **man**: "You are free to eat
from any tree in the garden. But
the Tree of Knowledge of **good
and bad** – you may not eat from
that, for on the day you eat from
it, you will surely die." (Bereshit
2:16–17)

סוֹף דָּבָר הַכֹּל נִשְׁמָע אֶת־הָאֱלֹהִים
יְרָא וְאֶת־**מִצְוֹתָיו** שְׁמוֹר כִּי־זֶה
כָּל־**הָאָדָם**. כִּי אֶת־כָּל־מַעֲשֶׂה
הָאֱלֹהִים יָבֹא בְמִשְׁפָּט עַל כָּל־נֶעְלָם
אִם־**טוֹב וְאִם־רָע**.

The final word: it has all been
said. Fear **God** and keep His
commandments! For this is
the whole of **man**. For God will
bring every deed to judgment,
even hidden ones, whether
good or bad. (Kohelet 12:13–14)

In the final verses of Kohelet, Adam looks back and considers the
original commandment God gave in the Garden. Both verses have
"God," "command," "man" (both use the specific term *ha'adam*, literally, "the man" or "the Adam"), and "good and bad." With regret,
Adam says that had he feared God and followed His commandment, all that came to pass would not have occurred. As a result
of his disobedience, he was exiled from the Garden and death was
introduced into the world – the consequence of which would be
felt by all in future generations, even those more righteous than
he. Adam came to realize that God calls everyone to justice. Any
attempts to hide from God will fail.[4]

This is "the final word," says Kohelet, a warning to all those
hearing it, written with the hope that they will not make the same
mistake.

---

4. See Bereshit 3:8–9.

Chapter 8

Why the Name Hevel?

W e have made a connection between the noun *hevel* and the name of Adam's son Hevel. But if *hevel* means "futility" or "vanity," then why would Adam give his son that name? An even more basic meaning of *hevel* is "breath,"[1] whose transient nature also recalls futility. But naming a child "breath" is not any easier to understand.

It is true that Hevel's life did end in a futile manner, and there are other examples in the Tanakh of people with names reflecting their future destinies. For example, in the book of Rut, we read that Elimelekh's sons were named Maḥlon and Kilyon. One possible translation of those names could be "disease" and "destruction," and as the Midrash states,[2] their names foreshadowed their fate: They were erased and destroyed from the world (as they die without children at the beginning of the story).

---

1. See, for example, Yeshayahu 57:13; Mishlei 21:6.
2. *Rut Rabba* 2:5.

However, there are positive translations of the names Maḥlon and Kilyon, such as "Sweetness" and "Perfection,"[3] which could have been their parents' intent when they named their sons. Thus, the intention of the one who gives the name does not necessarily guarantee the outcome of a person's life.[4]

Considering this, the following is an explanation for why Hevel was given that name at birth:

The Midrash[5] claims that Kayin and Hevel were twins, noting that it says only once that Ḥava was pregnant, but twice that she gave birth: "The man knew his wife, Ḥava, and she conceived and gave birth to Kayin.... She then gave birth to his brother Hevel" (Bereshit 4:1–2). This is a reasonable conclusion; there are other prominent twins in Bereshit, and it would make sense that the first brothers would be a prototype for them.

We also know that carrying twins, and particularly their birth, was exceedingly difficult in those days.[6] After Kayin was born, out came another baby. Adam and Ḥava must have been shocked; could another baby survive? It might not have been clear if he was even breathing. But then he did breathe – and he was alive. He had *hevel* (breath)! His parents celebrated the birth of their second son by giving him a name celebrating his life against the odds.

Breath itself can be viewed as miraculous. Like the initial miracle of God breathing life into Adam, Kohelet notes the wondrous nature of babies being able to breathe:[7] "Just as you do not know how the life-breath passes into the body [of the fetus] within the

---

3. Feivel Meltzer, "Rut" in *Daat Mikra: Ḥamesh Megillot* (Jerusalem: Mossad Harav Kook, 1990), 1:2.
4. Ibid.
5. *Bereshit Rabba* 22:3.
6. Reflecting God's curse to the woman: "I will make your pain in pregnancy searingly great; in sorrow will you bear children" (Bereshit 3:16).
7. See *Kohelet Rabba* 11:5.

womb of the pregnant woman, so you cannot know the work of God; and everything is His work" (Kohelet 11:5).

Hevel continued to surprise everyone and defy the odds by being a rebel, a shepherd. He was full of breath, full of life.

After his murder, however, his name took on a much more sinister meaning. It still meant "breath," but once that breath was gone, it showed just how pointless life and breath really are. Just because you are breathing one moment doesn't mean you'll be breathing the next. As Kohelet puts it:

> Man [*adam*] has no power over the life-breath – he cannot cage up the life-breath; no one rules on the day of death, no one will take your place in that battle, and evil provides no escape for its masters. (Kohelet 8:8)

Adam had no power over the life-breath; he could not save Hevel on his day of death.

Chapter 9

To Everything There Is a Season

Kohelet 3:1–8 is a well-known collection of verses outlining various human actions and their opposites. Some of the verbs mentioned in these verses have parallels in Bereshit:

לַכֹּל זְמָן וְעֵת לְכָל־חֵפֶץ תַּחַת הַשָּׁמָיִם: עֵת **לָלֶדֶת** וְעֵת **לָמוּת** עֵת
לָטַעַת וְעֵת לַעֲקוֹר נָטוּעַ: עֵת **לַהֲרוֹג** וְעֵת לִרְפּוֹא עֵת לִפְרוֹץ וְעֵת
לִבְנוֹת: עֵת לִבְכּוֹת וְעֵת לִשְׂחוֹק עֵת סְפוֹד וְעֵת רְקוֹד: עֵת לְהַשְׁלִיךְ
אֲבָנִים וְעֵת כְּנוֹס אֲבָנִים עֵת לַחֲבוֹק וְעֵת לִרְחֹק מֵחַבֵּק: עֵת לְבַקֵּשׁ
וְעֵת לְאַבֵּד עֵת **לִשְׁמוֹר** וְעֵת לְהַשְׁלִיךְ: עֵת לִקְרוֹעַ וְעֵת **לִתְפּוֹר** עֵת
לַחֲשׁוֹת וְעֵת לְדַבֵּר: עֵת לֶאֱהֹב וְעֵת לִשְׂנֹא עֵת מִלְחָמָה וְעֵת שָׁלוֹם:

Everything has its moment, a time for every action under heaven:

There is a time for **birth** and a time for **death**;

a time to **plant** and a time to uproot.
A time to **kill**, a time to heal;
a time to tear down and a time to **build** up.
A time to weep, a time to laugh;
a time for eulogy and a time for dance.
A time to cast away stones, a time to gather them up;
a time to embrace and a time to hold back from
    embracing.
A time to seek, a time to lose;
a time to **keep** and a time to cast aside.
A time to tear, a time to **sew**;
a time for silence and a time for speech.
A time to love, a time to hate;
a time for war and a time for peace. (Kohelet 3:1–8)

וְהָאָדָם יָדַע אֶת־חַוָּה אִשְׁתּוֹ וַתַּהַר וַתֵּלֶד אֶת־קַיִן וַתֹּאמֶר קָנִיתִי
אִישׁ אֶת־יְהֹוָה.

The man knew his wife, Ḥava, and she conceived and gave
birth to Kayin, saying, "With the Lord's help I have made
a man." (Bereshit 4:1)

וּמֵעֵץ הַדַּעַת טוֹב וָרָע לֹא תֹאכַל מִמֶּנּוּ כִּי בְּיוֹם אֲכָלְךָ מִמֶּנּוּ
מוֹת תָּמוּת.

But the Tree of Knowledge of good and bad – you may not
eat from that, for on the day you eat from it, you will surely
die. (2:17)

וַיִּטַּע יְהֹוָה אֱלֹהִים גַּן־בְּעֵדֶן מִקֶּדֶם וַיָּשֶׂם שָׁם אֶת־הָאָדָם אֲשֶׁר יָצָר.

The Lord God **planted** a garden in Eden, in the east, and
there he put the man He had formed. (2:8)

74

וַיֹּאמֶר קַיִן אֶל־הֶבֶל אָחִיו וַיְהִי בִּהְיוֹתָם בַּשָּׂדֶה וַיָּקָם קַיִן אֶל־הֶבֶל
אָחִיו **וַיַּהַרְגֵהוּ.**

Kayin talked to his brother Hevel, and when they were in
the field, Kayin rose up against his brother Hevel and **killed**
him. (4:8)

וַיִּבֶן יְהוָה אֱלֹהִים אֶת־הַצֵּלָע אֲשֶׁר־לָקַח מִן־הָאָדָם לְאִשָּׁה וַיְבִאֶהָ
אֶל־הָאָדָם.

And God the Lord **built** the rib He had taken from the
man into a woman, and He brought her to the man. (2:22)

וַיֹּאמֶר יְהוָה אֶל־קַיִן אֵי הֶבֶל אָחִיךָ וַיֹּאמֶר לֹא יָדַעְתִּי **הֲשֹׁמֵר** אָחִי
אָנֹכִי.

The Lord asked Kayin, "Where is your brother Hevel?" "I
do not know," he said. "Am I my brother's **keeper**?" (4:9)

וַתִּפָּקַחְנָה עֵינֵי שְׁנֵיהֶם וַיֵּדְעוּ כִּי עֵירֻמִּם הֵם **וַיִּתְפְּרוּ** עֲלֵה תְאֵנָה
וַיַּעֲשׂוּ לָהֶם חֲגֹרֹת.

The eyes of both of them were opened, and they realized
that they were naked. So they **sewed** fig leaves together and
made coverings for themselves. (3:7)

As we can see, the verbs born, die, plant, kill,[1] build, keep, and
sew appear in both Kohelet and Bereshit. But what about the

---

1. The Gaon of Vilna notes in his commentary on Kohelet here that Hevel was the first
person in the world to be killed, and thus, "a time for killing" refers to Hevel. Hevel
was also apparently the first person to kill an animal (for sacrifice), but in the end
there was no difference between him and them: "For the fate of man is the fate of
cattle: the same fate awaits them both, the death of one is like the death of the other,

other verbs mentioned in Kohelet? The following explanation is speculative.

Generally, the words in a text tell the narrative. But a sensitive reading of the above verses in Bereshit, aided by the parallel passage in Kohelet, may allow us to fill in the gaps. It is therefore possible that the other verbs in the Kohelet passage reveal what Adam felt or experienced. In this way, Kohelet is filling in the gaps, answering questions Bereshit does not address.

Using this approach, how might Adam have recalled the happier days before Hevel died? **Laughing** and **dancing**. How may Adam have reacted to Hevel's death? With **weeping**, with **tearing** his clothes, and sitting in **silence**.

We don't read about Adam's reaction to the murder. We may therefore speculate that Adam **searched** for his son Hevel, only to discover him **lost**. In the past, he could **embrace** his children, but now he **refrained from embracing** Kayin.

Even the stones from the verses in Kohelet may have relevance. Adam could have **gathered stones** to place on Hevel's grave,[2] and perhaps there is even a hint to how Kayin killed Hevel – by **casting a stone**.[3]

---

their life-breath is the same, and the preeminence of man over beast is nothing, for it is all futile [*hevel*]" (Kohelet 3:19).

2. There are several examples in the Tanakh of placing heaps of stones on graves; see Yehoshua 7:26, 8:29; Shmuel II 18:17.

3. This is the position of the Book of Jubilees (4:44): "With a stone he had killed Hevel." Death by stoning is mentioned frequently in the Tanakh. Moreover, the only other time in the Tanakh we find this particular language of throwing stones, it also ends in death:

וַיהוָה **הִשְׁלִיךְ** עֲלֵיהֶם אֲבָנִים גְּדֹלוֹת מִן־הַשָּׁמַיִם עַד־עֲזֵקָה וַיָּמֻתוּ – "The Lord hurled huge stones on them from the sky, all the way to Azekah, and they died" (Yehoshua 10:11).

Chapter 10

Why Did Shlomo Write This Way?

W e have shown much symmetry between the stories in the opening chapters of Bereshit and the book of Kohelet. Every additional parallel verse supports the thesis that this is no coincidence but was the intent of Kohelet's author. And yet, the question remains: Why did Shlomo write in such a perplexing way? What do we gain from correlating the Adam and Shlomo stories?

The use of the exegetical method of intertextuality enhances our understanding of both stories. For example, the Adam story helps us understand what Shlomo was experiencing at the end of his life: pain and regret. Likewise, the book of Kohelet helps us understand the Adam story by showing us how responsible Adam felt for the death of Hevel.

Why does Shlomo not even include his own name in the book of Kohelet? Why isn't he more direct? Why not clearly state that the work is a reflection on Adam's life? Why not match the Bereshit story more precisely?

The puzzle-like nature of the book, requiring effort to reassemble and decipher the hints, appears to be Shlomo's way of hiding the secret of his shame. Future generations will read the book, but it should not be immediately obvious that bound up in Israel's greatest hour was the source of its ultimate downfall.[1]

That said, the complex, even contradictory, nature of the book of Kohelet has caused some readers to question its content. For example, the Sages sought to hide it and remove it from the biblical canon because of its contradictory messages. Only because it begins and ends with words of Torah did they keep Kohelet in the Tanakh.[2]

Another difficulty with the book of Kohelet can be found in this verse: "I, Kohelet, was king of Israel in Jerusalem" (Kohelet 1:12). Some have claimed this proves Shlomo cannot be synonymous with Kohelet, for Kohelet says he *was* king, in the past, whereas Shlomo remained king his entire life. However, with our understanding of the book as a review of Shlomo's life, the verse makes sense. Shlomo had fallen from God's grace and wrote from the point of view of one who can no longer take pride in sitting on the throne.[3]

---

1. I suggest this is the reason Divrei HaYamim does not mention the story of Shlomo's sin or downfall at all (see Divrei HaYamim II, 9).
2. Shabbat 30b.
3. See above, chapter 3, note 2, for the midrashic interpretation of this verse.

Chapter 11

What's Wrong with the Search for Knowledge?

After a detailed review of the verses describing both Adam's life and Shlomo's life, the parallels are clear. One prominent parallel is their search for knowledge. Shlomo's desire for knowledge did not lead to the happiness he had hoped for. In Adam's case, as Kohelet describes it, the search for knowledge was the very cause of his downfall. Adam and Ḥava desired the fruit of the Tree of Knowledge, and when they succeeded in acquiring it, it led directly to their exile from the Garden and their divine punishments. If Shlomo saw his life as a reflection of Adam's, did he view his own search for knowledge as the root of his tragedy?

The answer can be found in this introductory verse[1] of Kohelet: "I gave my heart to seek and to search out with wisdom all

---

1. This verse can be seen as the opening of the book. Verses 1–11 of the first chapter serve as a preamble, and in verse 12, Kohelet introduces himself. Verse 13, therefore,

that happens under the heavens – an evil task that God gave men to be afflicted with [*la'anot bo*]"[2] (Kohelet 1:13).

Here, Shlomo is saying he dedicated his heart to the search for knowledge,[3] but it became an evil task. A related verse later in the book demonstrates Kohelet's regret regarding that search for knowledge:

סַבּוֹתִי אֲנִי וְלִבִּי לָדַעַת וְלָתוּר וּבַקֵּשׁ חָכְמָה וְחֶשְׁבּוֹן וְלָדַעַת רֶשַׁע
כֶּסֶל וְהַסִּכְלוּת הוֹלֵלוֹת:

I turned my heart from understanding and exploring, from seeking wisdom and reason; and from knowing wickedness, foolishness, folly, and madness. (Kohelet 7:25)[4]

Shlomo has despaired of his original search for knowledge. What led to this change of heart?

SHLOMO'S HEART OF WISDOM

Shlomo's heart[5] is a central element in both the writings about him and by him.

In Kohelet 1:13, Shlomo says he gave his (own) heart to study wisdom, but in Shlomo's first dialogue with God, he asks God for a heart: "Give Your servant a listening heart to judge Your people, to distinguish between good and bad; for who can judge this immense people of Yours?" (Melakhim I 3:9). He asks for a

---

presents the background to the rest of the book.

2. Following Ibn Ezra. Others translate *la'anot bo* as "to be concerned with."

3. See the commentary of R. Yeshaya de Trani to Kohelet 1:18. He notes that all "wisdom" mentioned in Kohelet is not the wisdom of Torah, but rather the "wisdom of knowledge."

4. This translation follows the explanation of Zer-Kavod in *Daat Mikra*.

5. In biblical times, the heart was viewed as the source of thought, and so some translate the Hebrew, *lev*, as "mind." While that better reflects the modern conception, for consistency's sake I will continue to translate it as "heart."

heart that listens and recognizes that God will give him the ability to distinguish between good and bad. In response, God gives him the heart he requested: "I give you a wise and understanding heart" (3:12).

However, in Mishlei (which we noted earlier is traditionally viewed as having been written in the middle of Shlomo's life), Shlomo presents a slightly different version of the source of his wisdom: "Happy is the man who found wisdom" (Mishlei 3:13). Here he says he "found" wisdom (instead of being given it by God).[6] While finding wisdom may be admirable for most people, Shlomo was privy to the understanding that true wisdom is a gift from God.

Later in that same chapter, he compares wisdom to a tree: "It is a tree of life for those who grasp it, those who hold fast to it are happy" (3:18). However, to Shlomo, this is not the forbidden Tree of Knowledge, but rather the alluring, out-of-reach, Tree of Life. This tree should make him happy – "those who hold fast to it are happy." Yet at the end of his life, his search for wisdom turns out to be a repeat of Adam's disastrous consumption of fruit of the Tree of Knowledge, and throughout Kohelet he is not happy:

> I said to my heart, I have gathered and built up more wisdom than anyone who has ruled over Jerusalem before, and my heart has seen[7] much of wisdom and insight. And I gave

---

6. A few verses later, we read: "Long life is in its [wisdom's] right hand; in its left hand is wealth and honor" (Mishlei 3:16). His association of wisdom with long life, wealth, and honor shows a distinctly different perspective from that which he had after his first dialogue with God (Melakhim I 3:5–14), in which he did not ask for those things. Perhaps at this point in his life, Shlomo took them for granted, like the wisdom he "found."

7. It is noteworthy that in this verse Shlomo describes a "seeing heart," whereas in the divine gift of wisdom, God gave him a "hearing heart." It is rare in the Tanakh to describe the heart as either seeing or hearing, so the contrast is marked. In biblical Hebrew, listening is identified with obedience, and as we shall see shortly, seeing is

my heart over to understand wisdom, to discern madness and folly. I know that too is pursuing the wind. For in great wisdom lies great bitterness; and one who gathers insight gathers pain. (Kohelet 1:16–18)

The arc of Shlomo's life can be tracked by how he feels he acquired that wise heart. If his heart is from God, then that would carry with it the humility not to challenge God. Later, he expresses the neutral idea that his heart was "found." But once it was something he gave to himself,[8] then he could easily do with it as he pleased. In Kohelet, he realizes he misused his gift. The same wisdom used to build the Temple for God was used later for diplomatic purposes that eventually led to idolatry. His heart did not listen to God, and he determined on his own what was good and what was evil.

It is significant that the Sages identified Mishlei's "tree of life" not with human wisdom, but with the divine Torah.[9] This interpretation redeems the verse from its problematic context in Shlomo's life and has granted it special status in our prayers today.[10]

---

often associated with disobedience and sin. By switching the specific sense associated with his heart, Shlomo admits he has altered its purpose.

8. See Kohelet 1:13, 8:16, and 9:1, where Shlomo says he literally "gave his heart."
9. See, for example, Avot 6:7; Berakhot 32b.
10. One other mention of the "tree of life" in Mishlei (13:12) sheds light on the nature of Shlomo's change of approach in Kohelet: "Hope deferred makes the heart sick, but fulfilled desire is a tree of life." In Mishlei, Shlomo writes that when one does not get what he hopes for, when his desires are not immediately fulfilled, the heart becomes sick; but when his desires are realized, it is as if he ate from the tree of life. In Kohelet, Shlomo reminds us over and over again that even when one thinks his wishes, whether for riches or for wisdom, are achieved, in the end it is all futility.

The Story of the Spies

Chapter 12

The Garden and the Spies

A s we mentioned in the introduction to this book, there is another biblical story that contains the same themes and linguistic clues as those found with Adam and Shlomo: the story of the spies. As we will see, this downfall is similar to those we have previously examined, and in this story the punishment led to an entire generation dying in the desert instead of entering the promised land. But there is much more to it than that.

Let's return to Kohelet. In 1:13, we find the interesting use of the Hebrew verb root T-O-R, "to search" (or "to seek"). This root rarely appears in the Tanakh but is found primarily in two books: Kohelet (three times) and Bemidbar, where it appears frequently in the story of the spies.[1] There it has the related connotation of "to scout," as we can see from the opening verse of the story: "Send for yourself men to scout [*veyaturu*] the land of Canaan, which I am going to give to the Israelites, one man from each of their ancestral tribes, each a leader among them" (Bemidbar 13:2).

---

1. Bemidbar 13:2, 16, 17, 21, 25, 32; 14:6, 7, 34, 36, 38.

The root T-O-R is used to signal common themes in different contexts. For example, in Kohelet it doesn't have any connotation of espionage, whereas in Bemidbar it was chosen deliberately over the root R-G-L, which only means "to spy" and not the more general "to search."

We find several interesting connections between the story of Adam in the Garden and the story of the spies in Bemidbar.[2] The structures of the stories are remarkably similar. Here are six prominent elements found in both:

- **A quest for knowledge of good and bad:** Adam and Ḥava ate from the tree that gave them knowledge of good and bad, and the spies went to determine whether the land was good or bad.
- **Acquisition of fruit:** Adam and Ḥava took fruit from the tree, and the spies took fruit back from the land.
- **Ignoring God's command:** In both stories, the protagonists did not listen to God.
- **Punishment by death, where the immediate death penalty is delayed:** Adam was told that the day he ate from the tree he would die (Bereshit 2:17), but in the end, while he was subject to death, it only happened hundreds of years later. God initially planned on immediately killing the generation of the spies (Bemidbar 14:12), but after Moshe's petition, decreed they die over the next forty years (vv. 33–34).
- **Expulsion from/prohibition from entering God's land:** Adam and Ḥava were expelled from the Garden, and the generation of the spies were prohibited from entering the Land.

---

2. R. Samson Raphael Hirsch on Bemidbar 15:41 comments that the sins are not just connected and similar but are essentially the same.

- **Entry to land prevented by sword:** After expelling Adam from the Garden, God placed cherubim with swords to prevent his return. After the punishment of the generation of the spies, those who tried to enter the Land fell by the swords of the Amalekites and Canaanites (Bemidbar 14:43–45).

Looking at the verses themselves, we can see that the narrative symmetry is reinforced by linguistic parallels:

וּמֵעֵץ הַדַּעַת **טוֹב וָרָע** לֹא תֹאכַל מִמֶּנּוּ כִּי בְּיוֹם אֲכָלְךָ מִמֶּנּוּ מוֹת תָּמוּת.	וּמָה הָאָרֶץ אֲשֶׁר־הוּא יֹשֵׁב בָּהּ **הֲטוֹבָה** הִוא אִם־**רָעָה** וּמָה הֶעָרִים אֲשֶׁר־הוּא יוֹשֵׁב בָּהֵנָּה הַבְּמַחֲנִים אִם בְּמִבְצָרִים.
But the Tree of Knowledge of **good and bad** – you may not eat from that, for on the day you eat from it, you will surely die. (Bereshit 2:17)	Is the land in which they live **good or bad**? Are the towns in which they live open or fortified? (Bemidbar 13:19)

Both verses have the phrase "good and bad," and in both cases, humans pursue knowledge of "good and bad."

וַתֵּרֶא הָאִשָּׁה כִּי טוֹב **הָעֵץ** לְמַאֲכָל וְכִי תַאֲוָה־הוּא לָעֵינַיִם וְנֶחְמָד **הָעֵץ** לְהַשְׂכִּיל **וַתִּקַּח מִפִּרְיוֹ** וַתֹּאכַל וַתִּתֵּן גַּם־לְאִישָׁהּ עִמָּהּ וַיֹּאכַל.	וּמָה הָאָרֶץ הַשְּׁמֵנָה הִוא אִם־רָזָה הֲיֵשׁ־בָּהּ **עֵץ** אִם־אַיִן וְהִתְחַזַּקְתֶּם **וּלְקַחְתֶּם מִפְּרִי הָאָרֶץ** וְהַיָּמִים יְמֵי בִּכּוּרֵי עֲנָבִים.
The woman saw that the **tree** was good for eating, enticing to the eyes, and desirable too for granting intelligence. She **took some of its fruit** and ate, and she gave some to her husband and he too ate. (Bereshit 3:6)	"Is the soil rich or poor? Are there **trees** in it or not? Take courage and **take some of the fruit** of the land." It was the season of the first ripe grapes. (Bemidbar 13:20)

Here, both verses mention trees,[3] but even more noteworthy are the phrases used to describe the taking of fruit. In the entire Torah, only on very few occasions are the verb L-K-Ḥ and the noun *pri* found together in the same verse. Besides the two cited here, there is one in Devarim (1:25) when Moshe recounts the story of the spies, and two others relating to commandments that involve the taking of fruit: the four species of Sukkot (Vayikra 23:40) and the offering of the first fruits (Devarim 26:2).[4]

וּלְאָדָם אָמַר כִּי־שָׁמַעְתָּ לְקוֹל אִשְׁתֶּךָ וַתֹּאכַל מִן־הָעֵץ אֲשֶׁר צִוִּיתִיךָ לֵאמֹר לֹא תֹאכַל מִמֶּנּוּ אֲרוּרָה הָאֲדָמָה בַּעֲבוּרֶךָ בְּעִצָּבוֹן תֹּאכְלֶנָּה כֹּל יְמֵי חַיֶּיךָ.	כִּי כָל־הָאֲנָשִׁים הָרֹאִים אֶת־כְּבֹדִי וְאֶת־אֹתֹתַי אֲשֶׁר־עָשִׂיתִי בְמִצְרַיִם וּבַמִּדְבָּר וַיְנַסּוּ אֹתִי זֶה עֶשֶׂר פְּעָמִים וְלֹא שָׁמְעוּ בְּקוֹלִי.
To Adam He said, "Because **you listened to the voice of your wife** and ate of the tree from which I commanded you not to eat – cursed will be the land on your account. With anguish you will eat from it all the days of your life." (Bereshit 3:17)	None of those who have seen My glory and the signs I performed in Egypt and in the wilderness, and who have tested Me these ten times and **not listened to My voice**. (Bemidbar 14:22)

From these verses we see that neither Adam nor the generation of the spies listened to the voice of God.

---

3. Interestingly, the verse in Bemidbar has the singular *etz*, tree, so literally the question was, "Is there a tree in it or not?" While the singular form of the word can refer to a collective group of trees, the choice of language here strongly alludes to the time in the Garden when only one tree had a particular restriction.
4. One could posit that these two commandments are meant to teach the people that fruit should be taken in the proper framework, as part of the service of God.

וַיְגָרֶשׁ אֶת־הָאָדָם וַיַּשְׁכֵּן מִקֶּדֶם לְגַן־עֵדֶן אֶת־הַכְּרֻבִים וְאֵת לַהַט הַחֶרֶב הַמִּתְהַפֶּכֶת לִשְׁמֹר אֶת־דֶּרֶךְ עֵץ הַחַיִּים.	כִּי הָעֲמָלֵקִי וְהַכְּנַעֲנִי שָׁם לִפְנֵיכֶם וּנְפַלְתֶּם בֶּחָרֶב כִּי־עַל־כֵּן שַׁבְתֶּם מֵאַחֲרֵי יְהוָה וְלֹא־יִהְיֶה יְהוָה עִמָּכֶם.
He drove out the man, and east of the Garden of Eden He placed the cherubim and the flaming, whirling **sword** to guard the way to the Tree of Life. (Bereshit 3:24)	Ahead of you are the Amalekites and Canaanites, and you will fall by the **sword**. Because you have turned away from following the Lord, the Lord will not be with you. (Bemidbar 14:43)

Both verses describing the barriers of entry to God's land include the sword as the means of preventing such a trespass.

TRUE OR GOOD?

All the parallels above, and particularly the use of the keyword T-O-R, lead to the conclusion that both Adam and the spies failed in their quest for knowledge. Earlier, we explored why Shlomo's search for knowledge led to his downfall. But what was inherently wrong with Adam eating the fruit? Why was it improper for the spies to report on the land?

A closer look at these two stories will help us find an answer.

In the Garden narrative, it is prohibited to eat from the Tree of Knowledge of good and bad. But surely a book as dedicated to proper, moral behavior as the Torah cannot possibly be discouraging the acquisition of knowledge of what is good and what is bad! A subsequent verse paints a different picture of the nature of that tree:

> The Lord God then said, "Now that man has become like one of us, knowing good and bad, he must not be allowed to reach out his hand and take also from the Tree of Life, eat, and live forever." (Bereshit 3:22)

Here God is concerned that man will be like Him, knowing good and bad. But the difference between man and God is not in *knowledge* of good and bad, but in *determining* what is good and what is bad. This ability to discern is not an objective understanding of what is proper, but rather a subjective one.

The distinction between these two types of knowledge was elaborated upon by Maimonides in the opening chapters of *Guide for the Perplexed*. He differentiates between the knowledge of "true and false" and "good and bad":

> Man, by virtue of his intellect, knows truth from falsehood, and this holds true for all intelligible things.... However, when [Adam] disobeyed...he was punished by being deprived of that intellectual apprehension.... He had become absorbed in judging things to be bad or good.[5]

A similar issue arises with the sin of the spies. An objective mission to determine facts on the ground before entering the land[6] would not only have been acceptable, it would have been expected.[7] However, the spies did not remain objective. After giving their initial account, where they said the land was "indeed flowing with milk and honey" (Bemidbar 13:27), they began giving a subjective report:

> But the people who live in the land are fierce, and the towns are fortified and very large indeed. We even saw the descendants of Anak there....We cannot go up against those people, for they are stronger than us. (Bemidbar 13:28–31)

---

5. *Guide for the Perplexed* I:2.

6. As found in Yehoshua 2:1–24.

7. Although perhaps the people should have learned from Avraham, who went to the land without "knowing whether it was good or bad" (as pointed out by Radak on Bereshit 12:1).

Like Adam, the spies veered from a justified quest for knowledge of "true and false" to a subjective determination of "good and bad." And as in the story of the Garden, they acted like God, deciding on their own whether the mission to conquer the land would succeed. They were thus barred from entering the land, like Adam; but their children, who did not fail in the same sin – that is, determining good from bad – would enter:

וְטַפְּכֶם אֲשֶׁר אֲמַרְתֶּם לָבַז יִהְיֶה וּבְנֵיכֶם אֲשֶׁר לֹא־יָדְעוּ הַיּוֹם טוֹב וָרָע הֵמָּה יָבֹאוּ שָׁמָּה וְלָהֶם אֶתְּנֶנָּה וְהֵם יִירָשׁוּהָ:

As for your little ones, whom you thought would be taken captive, and your children who **do not yet know good and bad**, they shall enter, and I will give it to them, and they will take possession of it. (Devarim 1:39)

Chapter 13

Didn't God Order the Mission of the Spies?

A s we have presented it so far, the very mission of the spies was problematic. They were sent to scout out the land, with the special verb T-O-R, implying a subjective search for knowledge. Even before they set out, since their expedition was associated with a problematic mindset, it was not likely to succeed and should have been avoided. However, it was God who commanded that they embark on the mission: "The Lord spoke to Moshe: 'Send for yourself men to scout the land of Canaan'" (Bemidbar 13:1–2). If God ordered the mission, how can the people who carried out His mission be to blame?

There are several ways to approach this difficulty. First, a comparison should be made to a parallel passage in the first chapter of Devarim, where Moshe recounted what had happened in the previous forty years:

Then all of you drew close to me and said, "Let us send men ahead of us to explore the land and bring back a report to us about the route by which we should go up and the towns we will come to." The plan seemed good to me, so I selected twelve of you, one man from each tribe. (Devarim 1:22–23)

According to Moshe's words in the book of Devarim, the request to send the spies came from the people, not from God. Rashi resolves this apparent contradiction by noting that in Bemidbar 13:2, God says, "Send *for yourself.*" Rashi says this was a message to Moshe that he should send the spies:

According to your own judgment. I do not command you, but if you wish to do so, send them. God said this because the Israelites came to Moshe and said, "Let us send men ahead etc.," as it is stated (Devarim 1:22), "Then all of you drew close to me [and said, "Let us send men]," and Moshe took counsel with God, whereupon He said to them, I have told them long ago that it (the land) is good, as it is stated (Shemot 3:17), "I will bring you up out of the misery of Egypt... [to a land flowing with milk and honey]."[1]

From here we see that while God conceded to the mission, He was not the one who instigated it, and in fact thought it was misguided. And in the end, God was correct; the spies did not provide an objective report, but rather a subjective judgment, and the nation believed them.

Abrabanel[2] goes one step further and writes that Moshe sinned by adding to God's original instruction in Bemidbar 13. God said only to send the mission, and later Moshe added the detail that

1. Rashi on Bemidbar 13:2.
2. Devarim 1:34.

they should investigate the nature of the land, including whether it was good or bad. Again, if Moshe was responsible for changing the nature of the mission, God's commandment is no longer problematic.

T-O-R AND TORAH

Yet, one question remains. Why did God use the loaded verb T-O-R in His commandment to Moshe? One answer is that He was expecting the leadership to follow the guidance from a few chapters earlier: "They journeyed from the Lord's mountain for three days; and the Ark of the Lord's Covenant went ahead of them for those three days to seek out [*latur*] a resting place for them" (Bemidbar 10:33). The verb root used to describe the "seeking out" of the Ark of the Covenant is the same special root we have been discussing: T-O-R. Here in Bemidbar 10, the Ark of the Covenant serves to remind the Israelites (and us) that God's Torah, and not our own rationalizations and considerations, should be our guide.[3] Moreover, I propose there is a play on words here between the words T-O-R (תור) and *Torah* (תורה). *Torah*, like T-O-R, is an odd word. It clearly derives from *horeh*, "instruct," the *hifil* form of the root Y-R-H, but it has an unusual format and is certainly a word of great significance. In the Tanakh, it refers only to divine (or religious) law.

The keyword T-O-R is used in the story of the spies and the subsequent laws of tzitzit to indicate following one's heart, while *Torah* refers to obeying the command of God.

The spies, and in their wake the entire nation, chose to follow their own hearts instead of what the Ark represented. This can also be seen from the story of the "defiant ones" (the *maapilim*)

---

3. It is noteworthy that the Ark appears more than twice as many times in verses mentioning David than it does in verses mentioning Shlomo. This is surprising, since the Ark was the centerpiece of the Temple Shlomo built. However, it seems the Ark was not as central to Shlomo's heart as it was for his father, David.

which immediately follows both God's punishment of the spies and the decree that the entire generation would die in the desert.

The *maapilim* were a group of people who decided to enter the land on their own, defying the decree that the generation of the desert would not enter the land. Moshe warned them, but they did not listen. When they marched into the land, the Amalekites and Canaanites soundly defeated them.[4] The brazenness and futility of their attempt is described as follows: "Defiantly, they went up to the heights of the hill country. Neither the **Ark of the Lord's Covenant** nor Moshe left the camp" (Bemidbar 14:44).

As we saw in Bemidbar 10, the Ark, and not the people's own ambitions, was intended to guide them. Even though the "defiant ones" appear to be the opposite of the spies – the latter opposed conquering the land, while the *maapilim* were convinced they would triumph – in the end, both followed their own hearts. Consequently, neither would succeed. They would not allow the Ark, and what it represented, to lead them.[5]

The key to success is formulated in the words of the mishna: "Fulfill His will as you would your own will, so that He may fulfill your will as though it were His will."[6]

When we fulfill His will as our own will, there is a convergence of T-O-R and Torah.

GOD IS THE TRUE JUDGE

After our examination of objective knowledge versus subjective evaluation, we can now examine a related thread common to all three stories – who is the real judge?

Shlomo asked for wisdom from God to properly judge his people, and his first test of that wisdom (the case of the two mothers)

---

4. Bemidbar 14:40–45.
5. Interestingly, the Ark is not mentioned in the rest of the nation's journeys. The next time it appears is in Yehoshua 3:3.
6. Avot 2:4.

showed the nation that he was indeed a wise judge. However, over time, Shlomo's wisdom came to be attributed to him, not to God, and Shlomo began to judge the validity and relevancy of God's commandments. By usurping God's role as ultimate Judge, Shlomo failed in the role assigned to him.[7] Our Sages[8] find a hint to this in the last chapter of Kohelet: "Kohelet sought to find words of delight; and words of truth written honestly" (Kohelet 12:10).

According to its rabbinic interpretation, this verse shows divine displeasure toward Shlomo's approach. The first half of the verse (seeking "words of delight") refers to Shlomo's inclination for issuing judgments of the heart based solely on his intuition, without witnesses and without warning. The second half of the verse ("words of truth"), the Sages assert, was spoken to Shlomo by a

---

7. In the book of Devarim, the king is not intended to act as a judge at all. Judges (*shoftim*) are mentioned in 16:18–20 and 17:8–13 (together with the priests, who can also judge). The king is discussed in the following section (17:14–20), but there is no mention of him acting as a judge at all. This is the approach of Ibn Kaspi on Shmuel I 8:6.

In the prophet Shmuel's time, the people ask for a king, but in addition to the formula from Devarim 17:14 ("Set a king over me, like all the surrounding nations"), they ask for a king to *judge* them: "Appoint a king for us, to judge us (*leshoftenu*) like all other nations" (Shmuel I 8:5). While some translate the verb *leshoftenu* as "rule" or "govern," this is unlikely, since it comes right after a discussion of Shmuel's sons, who were not judging the people with justice (Shmuel I 8:2–3). Shmuel is upset about the people's request for a king (8:6), and according to Ran (*Derashot HaRan* 11; see also Ralbag on Shmuel I 8:4), his anger was because they said, "Give us a king to *judge* us."

Certainly, kings do act as judges, but this role is not included in the Torah's plan for the king. And while David acted as a judge in Shmuel II, 14, his son Avshalom indicates in the following chapter that David was not focused on the task. Avshalom would tell people who were looking for judgment, "Your claim is right and just…. If only I were appointed judge…I would see that [everyone] got his rights." In this way, "Avshalom stole the hearts of the people of Israel" (Shmuel II 15:2–6).

Avshalom used his interest in judgment as a way of promoting himself as the rightful king. This darkly foreshadows the path of his brother Shlomo, who upon taking the throne also won the hearts of the people by being a judge. But since this is not the position assigned to the king, it led both brothers down a dangerous path.

8. Rosh Hashana 21b.

divine voice regarding his practice of deciding on the death penalty without the testimony of at least two witnesses (see Devarim 17:6).[9]

Shlomo was not the first to fail in this regard. As we have seen, the spies also did not understand the scope of their mission. They acted as judges, deciding what was good and bad, even when God had already determined the land to be good.

This trend of humans to act as judges instead of accepting God's judgment goes all the way back to the Garden. When Ḥava examined the tree, the Torah notes that "The woman saw that the tree **was good** (*ki tov*) for eating" (Bereshit 3:6). She and Adam acted as judges, deciding that the tree was "good for eating," despite the decision by God that of all the trees, this one was specifically not intended for them to eat.[10] The words used to describe her assessment of the tree echo the refrain found on each day of Creation in the first chapter of Bereshit: "And God saw that it **was good** (*ki tov*)."[11] Similar to Shlomo and the spies, Ḥava overstepped her bounds by acting like God. Before tasting the fruit, even before taking it, she had already failed to realize the difference between God and man.

God is the ultimate Judge of what is good and what is bad. As part of His partnership with mankind, God enables, encourages, and even requires humans to execute judgment on His behalf. To help with that goal, God grants humans the wisdom necessary

---

9. R. Zvi Hirsch Chajes, in his commentary on this talmudic passage, says the Sages' criticism of Shlomo stems from his judgment of the two mothers. Instead of basing his decision on the testimony of witnesses, as is required by the Torah, Shlomo relied on his own wisdom. Ralbag on Shmuel I 8:4 writes that this is precisely the danger of having a king who "will judge us." He will determine his own laws instead of following those laid down in the Torah. Therefore, as a preventive measure, the king must carry a Torah scroll with him at all times to recall the obligation to follow the Torah's laws, not his own.

10. R. Samson Raphael Hirsch on Bemidbar 15:41.

11. Rabbi David Fohrman, Aleph Beta video, "Eicha and Ayekah: Was There a Tisha B'Av in Eden?" https://www.alephbeta.org/playlist/megillat-eicha-and-ayekah-in-eden.

to be effective judges. But while acting as judges, humans need to remember that both their wisdom and their authority derive from God.

Shlomo fully understood this lesson when he composed Kohelet at the end of his life, and thus referred to God only by the divine name *Elohim*. While other names of God express distinct aspects of God's interaction with the world, *Elohim* describes God as Judge.[12] By exclusively using this name, Shlomo acknowledged that God is the true Judge.

Recognizing divine authority and the obligation to follow God's commandments is a key message of Kohelet. The book ends with this resolute declaration: "The final word: it has all been said. Fear God and keep His commandments! For this is the whole of man" (12:13).

Why do we need these "external" rules? Isn't it sufficient for everyone to follow their own moral conscience?

The Torah acknowledges that it is critical that everyone listen to their inner voice and act morally even in the absence of explicit commandments. Still, it is replete with examples of individuals, even the righteous, who when attempting to follow their conscience are corrupted by rationalization. They tell themselves that they are exempt from the established rules for noble reasons, yet too often are actually being led by their own, self-serving justifications.

---

12. There are biblical verses where the term *Elohim* refers to a human judge, e.g. Shemot 21:6, 22:7–8. The tension between Elohim as describing a human versus as the divine Judge can be found in a group of verses from the book of Tehillim, which criticizes evil judges: "I once thought, 'You are divine beings [*Elohim*]; all of you are children of the Most High,' but you shall die like a man; you will fall like any prince. Arise, O God [*Elohim*], judge the earth, for all the nations are Your possession" (82:6–8). These judges, called *Elohim*, acted as if they were divine, but in the end, they will die like a man (*Adam*). The psalmist therefore asks for the true Judge to arise. This message could apply to both Adam and Shlomo.

Kohelet teaches us that listening only to ourselves is an extremely dangerous path. The snake convinced Adam and Ḥava to eat from the tree, the spies convinced the nation that the conquest of the land would not succeed, and Shlomo convinced himself that he could safely ignore the laws of the king. None thought they were rebelling for their own sake, but they were blind to the disaster that soon followed.

When we commit ourselves to following an external authority, "fearing God and keeping His commandments," we have an effective balance to the "evil inclination" that consistently tries to tell us what is good and what is bad.

Section Four

Wine

Chapter 14

Wine – The Fruit of Knowledge?

Τ here are many elements alluded to in the three stories that we have just explored. One of them is wine.

WINE IN THE GARDEN

In the story of the Garden, the identity of the forbidden fruit is never revealed. The Sages present several theories as to what species of fruit it is, but the most common one found in midrashic literature is that the Tree of Knowledge produced grapes, and the fruit supplied wine. For example, the Sages make a connection between the story of Noaḥ, whose wine-drinking is explicitly mentioned in the text of the Torah, and Adam:

> The Holy One, blessed be He, said to Noaḥ, "Noaḥ, shouldn't you have learned from Adam the first [man],

whose sole reason for [banishment from the Garden of Eden] was wine?" [This is] in accordance with [the opinion of] the one who says the tree from which Adam the first [man] ate was a grapevine. As it is taught: R. Meir says, "The tree from which Adam the first [man] ate was a grapevine."[1]

Why would wine be so frequently associated with the prohibited Tree of Knowledge? Of all the fruits, wine is the one most likely to change a person's consciousness and perception.[2] Drinking wine "permits" us to do things that we otherwise would be reluctant to do, which is a phenomenon similar to the problematic transformation from objective knowledge to subjective judgment we discussed earlier. An intoxicated person does not feel bound to comply with internal or external norms and obligations. This reflects the state of mankind, in its first rebellion against God.[3]

It should be made clear that a plain reading of the text of Bereshit does not clearly lead to the conclusion that the fruit of the Tree of Knowledge was grapes, and as noted, other theories as to the identity of the fruit have been proposed. But for our purposes, it is significant that Kohelet, reflecting on Adam's life, does seem to agree with the identification of wine as the forbidden fruit:

---

1. Sanhedrin 70a.
2. The Talmud states, "One is obligated to become intoxicated [with wine] on Purim until he [is so intoxicated] that he does not know [how to distinguish] between 'cursed is Haman' and 'blessed is Mordekhai.'" (Megilla 7b). Considering the identification of the forbidden fruit with wine, this passage takes on new meaning. When tasting the fruit of the forbidden Tree of Knowledge of Good and Evil, Adam thought he was gaining knowledge, but in fact, he did not know the difference between good and evil at all. The same can be said of many who consume alcohol.
3. Uriel Eitam, *VeNahar Yotzeh Me'Eden – Shorsheihem shel Moadei HaShana beFarashat Gan Eden: Rosh Hashana, Yom Kippur, Sukkot* (Yeruḥam: Yeshivat HaHesder Yeruḥam, 2018), 152.

I searched [*tarti*] with my heart to tempt [*limshokh*] my flesh with wine and to grasp folly, while leading my heart with wisdom, that I might finally see what was good for men to do in their few days of life under heaven. (Kohelet 2:3)

Two Hebrew words in the verse are significantly connected to Adam. One is the word *tarti*, "searched," derived from the root T-O-R, which we addressed in the previous section. While that root does not appear in the Garden story, its connotation resonates strongly based on the parallels we have seen, particularly together with a mention of the heart. The other word, *limshokh*, "to tempt," literally means "to pull." It often has the sense of pulling in order to take an object.[4] While this word also does not appear in the Garden text, by using it here, Kohelet provides an image of pulling grapes (wine) off the branch, just as Ḥava did in the Garden.

WINE AND THE SPIES

In the story of the spies, grapes play a role as well. We mentioned that one of the parallels between the Garden and the spies was the taking of fruit. When Moshe commanded the spies to take fruit from the land, the Torah notes: "It was the season of the first ripe grapes" (Bemidbar 13:20). Grapes were the most significant fruit brought back by the spies: "Then they came to the Eshkol Ravine and there they cut down a vine branch, and on it one cluster of grapes, which they carried on a pole between two men. They also took some pomegranates and figs" (13:23).

It is noteworthy that following the episode of the spies, God gave several commandments that serve as consolation for not entering the land (all beginning with the promise, "When you enter the land..."). One of those commandments is the obligation to bring wine libations to accompany the ritual sacrifices:

---

4. For example, Bereshit 37:28 and Shemot 12:21.

> With the burnt offering or the sacrifice, a quarter of a hin of
> wine as a libation for every lamb ... a third of a hin of wine
> as a libation, for a pleasing aroma to the Lord ... You shall
> also offer half a hin of wine as a libation; it is a fire offering,
> a pleasing aroma to the Lord. (Bemidbar 15:5–10)

Since the commandments in this section are in response to the
preceding story of the spies, it can be understood that the use of
wine with the sacrifices comes to rectify the sin of the spies, associated with grapes. The Sages connect the commandments with
this consolation via a midrash on Kohelet. The verse states: "Go,
eat your bread in joy, drink your wine with a satisfied heart, for
God has already accepted your deeds" (Kohelet 9:7).

The midrash interprets the verse as follows:[5]

> "Go, eat your bread in joy": This is the commandment of
> separating the dough.
> "Drink your wine with a satisfied heart": This is the com-
> mandment of libations.
> "For God has already accepted your deeds": This is enter-
> ing the Land of Israel, as it says, "When you enter the
> land." (Bemidbar 15:2)

WINE AND SHLOMO

In the last of the three stories, wine is consumed freely during
the reign of King Shlomo: "Yehuda and Israel were as boundless
as the sand upon the seashore, eating and drinking and content"
(Melakhim I 4:20). Wine appears frequently in Shlomo's earliest
book, Shir HaShirim, as an allegory for love. For example, "Better
than any wine is your love" (Shir HaShirim 1:2). However, at the

---

5. *Bemidbar Rabba* 17:2.

end of the book of Mishlei, the purpose of wine is described in a very pointed manner:

> The words of King Lemuel, the oration with which his mother admonished him.... This is not for kings, Lemuel. It is not for kings to drink wine, nor for noblemen to ask, "Where is aged wine?" Lest they drink and forget what is inscribed and subvert the cause of all the downtrodden. Leave aged wine for the bereaved and wine for embittered souls. Let them drink and forget their poverty and never again remember their plight. (Mishlei 31:1–7)

Lemuel is an unidentified king, but since the book of Mishlei is attributed to Shlomo, the commentators say that Lemuel was Shlomo.[6] Whether Lemuel and Shlomo are the same person or not, the connection of these verses to Shlomo's life, and the role of wine in it, are clear. According to Mishlei, wine is for those who are suffering and impoverished. It is not for the king,[7] whose task is to enact justice. Wine's effect on the ruler will cause a loss of proper judgment, and, as we have learned, in the end Shlomo did oppress the people.

The Talmud (immediately following the section identifying the Tree of Knowledge with the grapevine) interprets the above verses in Mishlei as describing an interaction between Shlomo and his mother, Batsheva. According to this midrash, Batsheva

---

6. Rashi and Ibn Ezra on Mishlei 31:1. In addition, the verse omitted in the quotation, "Do not give your strength to women; nor your paths to those who destroy kings" (Mishlei 31:3), provides further reason to associate Lemuel with Shlomo, since his relationship with women is what destroyed his kingship.
7. Maimonides, in *Mishneh Torah, Hilkhot Melakhim* (3:5), adds drinking excessive wine to the prohibitions of amassing wives, horses, and gold that are explicitly mentioned in the Torah.

saw Shlomo engaged in excessive drinking, and castigated him. It then continues:

> R. Yitzḥak says: From where [can it be learned] that Shlomo repented and admitted to his mother [that she was justified in her rebukes]? As it is written: "For I am more foolish than a man, and have not the understanding of a man" (Mishlei 30:2). [This should be understood as follows:] "For I am more foolish than a man [*ish*]"; [that is, I am more foolish than Noaḥ, who sinned with wine and is called "a man"], as it is written: "And Noaḥ began to be a farmer [*ish ha'adama*]" (Bereshit 9:20). "And have not the understanding of a man [*adam*]"; this [is a reference to] Adam the first [man, who also sinned with wine, in accordance with the opinion of R. Meir, who says that the Tree of Knowledge was a grapevine].[8]

The Sages of the Talmud clearly state that Shlomo sinned with wine and note that Shlomo himself recognized that he followed the same pattern as Adam.[9] Rashi[10] writes that the excessive drinking that caused Shlomo's mother to get so upset happened when Shlomo married the daughter of Pharaoh.

The Sages also discuss that marriage in the following midrash, and go even further in describing the outcome of Shlomo's wine-drinking:

> R. Yudan said: All seven years that Shlomo was engaged in the building of the Temple he did not drink wine. After he built it, and married Pharaoh's daughter [in celebration],

---

8. Sanhedrin 70b.

9. Maharsha comments on the above passage that the reason Shlomo says he was more foolish than Adam and Noaḥ was that he should have learned from what happened to them.

10. Mishlei 31:1.

that night he drank wine. There were two excessive celebrations, one celebrating the building of the Temple and one celebrating the Pharaoh's daughter. God said, "Which [celebration] should I find acceptable, this [one] or that [one]?" At that moment, He considered destroying Jerusalem .... R. Ḥanina bar Papa said: God declared, "I had a large house and I destroyed it solely because of wine."[11]

Not only did wine lead to Shlomo's downfall, but it also led to the eventual destruction of Shlomo's most significant achievement – the building of the Temple in Jerusalem.

Kohelet could be referring to this aspect of Shlomo's life in the following two verses: "Happy the land whose king is a nobleman and whose princes eat at the right time, with restraint, without drunkenness" (Kohelet 10:17), in which he is praising a land where the leaders do not drink excessively, which is in contrast with Shlomo's kingdom; and in the verse, "I said in my heart, 'Come, let me treat [*anasekha*] myself with merriment; let me sate myself with good living.' I found that too was futile" (2:1). The merriment in this verse refers to drinking wine.[12] Shlomo thought it would bring him joy, but he later learned that it, too, was an unworthy pursuit.

In all three stories, wine was involved in a rebellion against God. However, wine is not solely negative. As Mishlei points out, when used in the right way, it can provide benefits. But it needs balance. It can allow you to forget your suffering but should not be used to ignore the suffering of others. It can lift up the hearts of

---

11. *Vayikra Rabba* 12:5.
12. Zer-Kavod in *Daat Mikra*, following Rashi and Ibn Ezra. The word *anaskha*, translated here as "treat," derives from the root N-S-KH, libations of wine, or M-S-KH, to pour wine.

the oppressed but should not allow you to "lift your heart above your brothers" (Devarim 17:20).[13]

In that manner, it can be redeemed from its association with betrayal of God by performing God's commandments – whether by the libations in the Temple, or in our time via the mitzvot that are performed with wine.

---

13. See Yirmeyahu 22:15, where King Yoshiyahu is described as one who "ate and drank and dispensed justice and righteousness, and then it was well with him." As Radak explains, even though he ate and drank in the manner of kings, because he also acted with justice and righteousness, all was well with him.

Section Five

Tzitzit

Chapter 15

The Commandment of Tzitzit

After exploring wine, an entity with negative connotations in all three stories, let us now look at a shared element with positive associations: tzitzit.

How do the parallels between the Garden story and the spies story help us understand Shlomo and Kohelet? The answer can be found in the Torah's epilogue to the spies story: the commandment of tzitzit. Comprising only a few verses, the tzitzit passage is loaded with intertextual links to other biblical passages, giving it much more meaning than its size suggests:

דַּבֵּר אֶל־בְּנֵי יִשְׂרָאֵל וְאָמַרְתָּ אֲלֵהֶם וְעָשׂוּ לָהֶם צִיצִת עַל־כַּנְפֵי בִגְדֵיהֶם לְדֹרֹתָם וְנָתְנוּ עַל־צִיצִת הַכָּנָף פְּתִיל תְּכֵלֶת. וְהָיָה לָכֶם לְצִיצִת וּרְאִיתֶם אֹתוֹ וּזְכַרְתֶּם אֶת־כָּל־מִצְוֹת יְהֹוָה וַעֲשִׂיתֶם אֹתָם וְלֹא־תָתוּרוּ אַחֲרֵי לְבַבְכֶם וְאַחֲרֵי עֵינֵיכֶם אֲשֶׁר־אַתֶּם זֹנִים אַחֲרֵיהֶם.

לְמַעַן תִּזְכְּרוּ וַעֲשִׂיתֶם אֶת־כָּל־מִצְוֹתָי וִהְיִיתֶם קְדֹשִׁים לֵאלֹהֵיכֶם.
אֲנִי יְהוָה אֱלֹהֵיכֶם אֲשֶׁר הוֹצֵאתִי אֶתְכֶם מֵאֶרֶץ מִצְרַיִם לִהְיוֹת לָכֶם
לֵאלֹהִים אֲנִי יְהוָה אֱלֹהֵיכֶם.

Speak to the Israelites and tell them to make for themselves fringes [tzitzit] on the **corners** of their garments[1]
throughout their generations; they should attach a cord
of blue [*tekhelet*] to each **corner** fringe. And this shall be
your fringe; **see** it and remember **all the commandments**
of God and observe them, so that you do not **seek** [*taturu*]
after your heart and **after your eyes**, which you **go astray**
[*zonim*] **after**. You will thus remember to observe **all My**
commandments and you will be holy to your God. I am
the Lord your God, who brought you out of Egypt to be
your God. I am the Lord your God. (Bemidbar 15:38–41)

The keyword that most clearly connects this passage to the
preceding story of the spies, as well as to the message in Kohelet, is *taturu*, from the root T-O-R. The Torah uses this verb to
describe the scouting of the spies, while the commandment of
tzitzit employs it to proscribe seeking after the temptations of
the senses. Thus, it stands to reason that tzitzit could have prevented the sin of the spies – and therefore the related sins of
Adam and Shlomo as well.

Another noteworthy word in the tzitzit passage is the verb
zonim in verse 39. The same verb root appears in the spies story:

וּבְנֵיכֶם יִהְיוּ רֹעִים בַּמִּדְבָּר אַרְבָּעִים שָׁנָה וְנָשְׂאוּ אֶת־זְנוּתֵיכֶם עַד־
תֹּם פִּגְרֵיכֶם בַּמִּדְבָּר.

---

1. The Hebrew word for "their garments," *bigdeihem*, appears only four times in the
entire Torah; one of them is here in the tzitzit passage and one appears in the spies
story (Bemidbar 14:6).

Your children will wander in the wilderness for forty years, suffering for your **going astray**, until the last of your corpses lies here in the wilderness. (Bemidbar 14:33)

The root z-n-h (זנה) indicates betrayal. Although it is translated as "go astray" here, this translation belies the harshness it connotes, as it typically refers to the severe sins of idolatry[2] or adultery.[3] Tzitzit is thus presented as a remedy to these grave transgressions. So, too, the use of t-o-r and z-n-h indicates that what seems to be a relatively minor practice – adding strings to a garment – actually plays a central role in rectifying serious offenses.

Even beyond the specific sins we just mentioned, the tzitzit passage says (twice) that those who wear tzitzit will remember and observe *all* of God's commandments. This provides an interesting parallel to the Garden story, where Adam and Ḥava also violated their commandment (which for them was *all* their commandments). But how can tzitzit do all that?

HEARTS AND EYES

A clue can be found in another key phrase in the tzitzit passage: the admonition against following "your heart and your eyes" (Bemidbar 15:39). Heart and eyes play major roles in the stories we have reviewed so far.

Eyes and seeing appear repeatedly in the story of the spies. We find it in their initial mission:

וּרְאִיתֶם אֶת־הָאָרֶץ מַה־הִוא וְאֶת־הָעָם הַיּשֵׁב עָלֶיהָ הֶחָזָק הוּא הֲרָפֶה הַמְעַט הוּא אִם־רָב.

See what the land is like. Are the people who live there strong or weak, few or many? (Bemidbar 13:18),

2. For example, Shemot 34:15–16; Vayikra 17:7, 20:5–6.
3. See Bereshit 38:24; Vayikra 21:7; Bemidbar 25:1.

as well as in the report they gave upon their return:

הָאָרֶץ אֲשֶׁר עָבַרְנוּ בָהּ לָתוּר אֹתָהּ אֶרֶץ אֹכֶלֶת יוֹשְׁבֶיהָ הִוא וְכָל־הָעָם
אֲשֶׁר־רָאִינוּ בְתוֹכָהּ אַנְשֵׁי מִדּוֹת. וְשָׁם רָאִינוּ אֶת־הַנְּפִילִים בְּנֵי עֲנָק
מִן־הַנְּפִלִים וַנְּהִי בְעֵינֵינוּ כַּחֲגָבִים וְכֵן הָיִינוּ בְּעֵינֵיהֶם.

The land that we journeyed through and scouted a land that
consumes its inhabitants; all the people that we **saw** in it
are men of great stature. There we **saw** the Nefilim – the
descendants of Anak are from the Nefilim. In our own **eyes**
we looked like grasshoppers, and so we were in their **eyes**.
(13:32–33)

Vision, too, plays a key role in the Garden story:

כִּי יֹדֵעַ אֱלֹהִים כִּי בְּיוֹם אֲכָלְכֶם מִמֶּנּוּ וְנִפְקְחוּ **עֵינֵיכֶם** וִהְיִיתֶם
כֵּאלֹהִים יֹדְעֵי טוֹב וָרָע . **וַתֵּרֶא** הָאִשָּׁה כִּי טוֹב הָעֵץ לְמַאֲכָל וְכִי
תַאֲוָה־הוּא **לָעֵינַיִם** וְנֶחְמָד הָעֵץ לְהַשְׂכִּיל וַתִּקַּח מִפִּרְיוֹ וַתֹּאכַל וַתִּתֵּן
גַּם־לְאִישָׁהּ עִמָּהּ וַיֹּאכַל. וַתִּפָּקַחְנָה **עֵינֵי** שְׁנֵיהֶם וַיֵּדְעוּ כִּי עֵירֻמִּם
הֵם וַיִּתְפְּרוּ עֲלֵה תְאֵנָה וַיַּעֲשׂוּ לָהֶם חֲגֹרֹת.

"God knows that on the day you eat from it your **eyes** will be
opened, and you will be like God, knowing good and bad."
The woman **saw** that the tree was good for eating, enticing to
the **eyes**, and desirable too for granting intelligence. She took
some of its fruit and ate, and she gave some to her husband
and he too ate. The **eyes** of both of them were opened, and
they realized that they were naked. So they sewed fig leaves
together and made coverings for themselves. (Bereshit 3:5–7)

In Shlomo's story, as we have discussed earlier, there is much more
focus on the heart. One passage that shows a connection to the
commandment of tzitzit occurs at the end of Shlomo's life:

King Shlomo loved many foreign women...from the nations of which the Lord had warned the Israelites: "You must not join with them, nor must they join with you, for they will turn your **hearts** astray **after** their own gods." Shlomo clung to these...and his wives turned his **heart** astray. By the time Shlomo grew old, his wives had turned away Shlomo's **heart** **after** other gods, and his **heart** was not entirely with the Lord, his God, as his father David's **heart** had been. Then the Lord raged against Shlomo, for his **heart** had turned away from the Lord, God of Israel, who had appeared to him twice and commanded him...not to follow **after** [*aharei*] other gods. But he failed to keep the Lord's command. (Melakhim I 11:1–4, 9–10)

In addition to the repetition of "heart," we find that the word *aharei,* "after," appears three times. *Aharei* is also found three times in the tzitzit passage: "Do not seek after your heart and after your eyes, which you go astray after." Instead of loving and clinging to God (as mandated in Devarim 11:22, 30:20), King Shlomo clung to and loved the forbidden women. This led him to idolatry, which as implied by the root z-n-h in the laws of tzitzit, is the inevitable outcome of such behavior.

Shlomo reflects on the problem of following heart and eyes twice in Kohelet:

I withheld from my **eyes** nothing that they asked for and denied my **heart** no enjoyment. For my **heart** rejoiced in the fruits of my labor, but this was all I got out of all my labor. (Kohelet 2:10)

Young man, rejoice now in your youth; let your **heart** give you pleasure while you are young. Follow your **heart** where it leads you, your **eyes** where they allure you – and know that God will bring you to judgment for all this. (11:9)

Shlomo gave his heart and his eyes whatever they desired, and at the time took immense pleasure in such a lifestyle. But at the end of his life, he looks back and sees he was left with nothing. He recognizes the young will enjoy themselves, following their hearts and their eyes. But he wants to make sure they know that when the time comes, as it did for him, God will judge all their actions.[4]

TZITZIT AND THE THREE STORIES

From what we have seen, the tzitzit passage relates to all three stories:

	T-O-R / Seeking	"After your heart and your eyes"	Z-N-H / Betrayal
Adam	Sought knowledge via the tree	Eyes	Disloyal to God – ate from the tree
Spies	Sought knowledge of the land	Eyes	Disloyal to God – gave a bad report of the land
Shlomo	Sought knowledge	Heart	Disloyal to God – idol worship

But while the problematic T-O-R/searching of Adam and the spies is clear, it is not obvious what was wrong with Shlomo's search

---

4. The Midrash (*Vayikra Rabba* 28:1) associates Shlomo's "Follow your heart where it leads you, your eyes where they allure you" with the Torah's "Do not seek after your heart and after your eyes." It finds the first half of the verse from Kohelet heretical, then congratulates Shlomo on the second half, i.e., "God will bring you to judgment for all this," as expressing the proper message.

(even though he explicitly mentions the dangers of searching for knowledge in Kohelet). If the focus is on a search for problematic knowledge, perhaps Shlomo's thirst for wisdom led him to a desire to know about the foreign cultures and religions that his many wives embodied. He got so caught up in it that he ended up trying all these manners of worship, which brought the punishment from God.

Looking at the two other stories, however, another picture emerges. Adam and Ḥava followed the snake's rationalizations and justified their eating from the prohibited tree. The spies, instead of providing objective intelligence, gave a subjective report. Furthermore, they recommended abandoning God's plan to enter the land and even suggested returning to Egypt. They all decided on their own what was right and what was wrong. Following this pattern, it wasn't Shlomo's objective search for knowledge that was problematic but rather his subjective rationalizations of God's commandments, particularly the restrictions on the king found in Devarim 17:16–7. As we noted earlier, according to the Sages,[5] Shlomo thought that the justifications given for those prohibitions did not apply to him, and so he ignored them – which eventually led to the disastrous idolatry and his downfall.

With this understanding of how the heart and eyes can lead to betrayal, we can return to our earlier question: How does the commandment of tzitzit prevent such serious concerns as presented in these three stories? The next chapter will explore this question.

---

5 Sanhedrin 21b.

Chapter 16

A Different Understanding of Tzitzit

It is difficult to accept that simply having extra strings on a garment would be sufficient to counter the sins mentioned in the stories of downfall we have been analyzing. Yet each story does have a connection to clothing. What does that indicate? Let's look at the function of garments in each one.

In the Garden story, Adam and Hava are not wearing clothes at all at first. However, once they realize they are naked, they make themselves clothes (from fig leaves), and later God makes them leather garments.

In the story of the spies, when Yehoshua and Kalev heard the people's defeatist response to the negative report, they tore their garments – a common expression of mourning in the Tanakh: "And Yehoshua son of Nun and Kalev son of Yefuneh, who were among those who had scouted the land, tore their clothes" (Bemidbar 14:6).

When God becomes angry with Shlomo for his betrayal, He presents Shlomo's punishment as follows:

וַיֹּאמֶר יְהוָה לִשְׁלֹמֹה יַעַן אֲשֶׁר הָיְתָה־זֹּאת עִמָּךְ וְלֹא שָׁמַרְתָּ בְּרִיתִי וְחֻקֹּתַי אֲשֶׁר צִוִּיתִי עָלֶיךָ **קָרֹעַ אֶקְרַע** אֶת־הַמַּמְלָכָה מֵעָלֶיךָ וּנְתַתִּיהָ לְעַבְדֶּךָ. אַךְ־בְּיָמֶיךָ לֹא אֶעֱשֶׂנָּה לְמַעַן דָּוִד אָבִיךָ מִיַּד בִּנְךָ **אֶקְרָעֶנָּה**. רַק אֶת־כָּל־הַמַּמְלָכָה לֹא **אֶקְרָע** שֵׁבֶט אֶחָד אֶתֵּן לִבְנֶךָ לְמַעַן דָּוִד עַבְדִּי וּלְמַעַן יְרוּשָׁלַם אֲשֶׁר בָּחָרְתִּי.

And the Lord said to Shlomo, "Because this has been your will, and you failed to keep My covenant and My laws, which I commanded you – I will surely **tear** the kingdom away from you, and I will give it to your servant. But for the sake of your father David, I will not do this in your own lifetime; I will **tear** it away from the hand of your son. And even so, I will not **tear** the whole kingdom away; I will grant a single tribe to your son for the sake of My servant David and for the sake of Jerusalem, which I have chosen." (Melakhim I 11:11–13)

God repeatedly says he will "tear" the kingdom from Shlomo. While He did not explicitly mention garments, that association is implied. In the story of Sha'ul, the last king to receive a remarkably similar message, the tearing of garments is symbolic of the tearing of the kingdom.[1] After the prophet Shmuel told King Sha'ul that God rejected him as king, Sha'ul begged, unsuccessfully, for forgiveness:

---

1. An additional story with kings and tearing is when the prophet Ahiya informs Shlomo's adversary Yorovam that he will be king (Melakhim I 11:29–39). Here, too, we find the tearing of a garment, but in this case, it indicates the giving of authority to Yorovam.

וַיִּסֹּב שְׁמוּאֵל לָלֶכֶת וַיַּחֲזֵק בִּכְנַף־מְעִילוֹ וַיִּקָּרַע. וַיֹּאמֶר אֵלָיו שְׁמוּאֵל קָרַע יְהוָה אֶת־מַמְלְכוּת יִשְׂרָאֵל מֵעָלֶיךָ הַיּוֹם וּנְתָנָהּ לְרֵעֲךָ הַטּוֹב מִמֶּךָּ.

And Shmuel turned to go, but Sha'ul grabbed the **corner of his robe, and it tore**. "The Lord has **torn** the kingship of Israel away from you today," Shmuel said to him, "and has granted it to your peer, who is better than you." (Shmuel I 15:27–28)

The imagery given to Shlomo and Sha'ul is almost identical. It is noteworthy that not only is the garment torn, but specifically the corner, *kanaf*, which appears in the passage of tzitzit as well.

HOW CAN TZITZIT HELP?

If we view tzitzit as we experience them today, as "extra strings on a garment," it is difficult to connect all these components. Let us see how the great medieval commentator Ibn Ezra can help us:

> **Make for themselves fringes [tzitzit]:** There are two possible interpretations. One, that they make tzitzit like those mentioned in Yeḥezkel 8:3, "*By the hairs [tzitzit] of my head,*" meaning they are the loose, unwoven threads [of the garment].

> **That shall be your tzitzit:** The second interpretation is as the Sages transcribed, and because they have reliable evidence, the first interpretation is canceled. And they passed on [the tradition] that the commandment applies when a garment has four corners.[2] And the tzitzit are the tassels, as I will explain [on Devarim 22:12]. This commandment applies to everyone who has a four-cornered garment, that

---

2. The mention of specifically four corners appears only in Devarim 22:12.

he should wear it during the day and not take it off, in order to remember. And those who wear a tallit during prayers do so because they recite the Shema, [which contains the verses] "that shall be your tzitzit" and "make for themselves tzitzit." But in my opinion, he is much more obligated to wear tzitzit during the rest of the day and not merely during prayers, in order to remember at all times not to err or commit a sin, since during prayers he will not commit a sin.[3]

In his first explanation, Ibn Ezra understands the meaning of the word tzitzit in light of the expression, "the tzitzit of my head," (i.e., my hair) in the book of Yeḥezkel, for tzitzit are like loose hairs from one's head. Following this understanding, tzitzit on a garment would be the unwoven strings on the edge [*kanaf*] of the fabric.[4] They are not added on, but part of the garment itself. (Not only a tallit, but any four-cornered garment requires tzitzit.)

In his second explanation, Ibn Ezra ultimately (and somewhat reluctantly)[5] rejects this opinion for the more traditional one that is in line with Jewish law,[6] but his first explanation, based

---

3. Ibn Ezra on Bemidbar 15:38–39.
4. Jacob Licht writes that *kanaf* actually means "edge (of a garment)," as understood from Ḥagai 2:12 (where it says people would carry meat in the *kanaf* of their garment, meaning "fold"), and other verses. (See *A Commentary on the Book of Numbers* II [Jerusalem: Magnes Press, 1991], 107.) This understanding fits well with the explanation of tzitzit as the "unwoven threads," which would be found all along the edge, not only on the corners.
5. Notice the way he finds fault with the traditional approach of wearing a tallit with tzitzit only during prayers, since at that time it is not likely to help much to avoid sin.
6. The two explanations are not mutually exclusive. We can still learn the lesson of the first explanation by viewing them as unfinished fringes, even when we manually add tzitzit to our garments. Moreover, we can learn important lessons from the literal or the alternative understanding of commandments in the Torah even if Jewish law does not follow that approach. For example, Jewish law clearly rules that "an eye for an eye" means monetary compensation, but the fact that the Torah uses the stronger

on a plain reading of the text, has much to offer.[7] As my teacher Shimon Heksher wrote,[8] the first explanation suggests tzitzit are not added on to a completed garment, but are rather the fringes of the unfinished edges of every garment we wear. Heksher said in this way it is like the commandment of *pe'ah* (Vayikra 19:9), where we are instructed to leave the four corners of the field unharvested.

This ties in perfectly with the stories we have seen earlier, particularly regarding the Garden. Just as the commandment of *pe'ah* teaches us that the field does not belong entirely to us, but rather the land is owned by God – "for the land is Mine" (Vayikra 25:23), so too does having unfinished corners of our garments remind us that they are not entirely our own possession, but were given to us by God.[9] One of the blessings we recite daily reminds us of this – *malbish arumim*: God "clothes the naked."

We first see that God gives us clothing at the end of the Garden story: "Then the Lord God made garments of skins for Adam and his wife and clothed them" (Bereshit 3:21).

From a visual perspective, our clothing is what most clearly distinguishes humans from animals. After eating from the tree, Adam and Ḥava realized the need for clothes, and despite their

---

language of "an eye for an eye" indicates there is a lesson to be learned about the severity of the injury from a simple reading of the text.

7. And if Ibn Ezra truly thought the first interpretation had no merit, he would simply never have mentioned it.

8. Shimon Heksher, *Va'ani Lo Bati Ela* (Ein Tzurim: Mishlabim, 2015), 312–313.

9. Heksher (ibid.) also points out that the *tekhelet* (the blue string) in the tzitzit was likely a sign of ownership, for in biblical times a slave wore a color indicating his owner. He writes that when the Torah mentions a slave having his ear pierced, the piercing itself wasn't the goal, but rather the dyed string placed in the hole indicating who the owner was. He also notes earlier (p. 32) that the sections in the Torah describing the covenant of the rainbow, the Passover offering, and the commandment of tzitzit all have the verbs R-A-H (see), N-T-N (give), and Z-KH-R (remember). All three thus indicate a covenant between man and God, and therefore the tzitzit are a sign that we are servants of God.

sin, God granted them clothing. There was no question for them that the garments they received were a divine gift.

For subsequent humans, that understanding is not so obvious. When we wear clothing, nothing about it seems unusual. A finished garment is logically the product of human hands – especially when we consider all the human effort required to produce clothing. But if we see tzitzit[10] as "loose hairs" on our garments, rendering our clothing unfinished and unusual, we will then understand that these are no normal garments. Rather, like Adam and Ḥava's clothing, they are commissioned by God. We will recall the events of the Garden and commit ourselves not to repeat the same sins. Tzitzit therefore provide that critical reminder of our actions and their consequences.

In chapter 12, we found six parallels between the story of the Garden and the story of the spies. There is a seventh. Both end with God giving clothing: Adam and Ḥava's garments after their expulsion from the Garden, and the tzitzit following the story of the spies.[11]

CLOTHING IN THE TANAKH

Understanding that clothing is not entirely our possession, but rather given to us by God, helps us clarify other difficult passages involving clothing in the Tanakh.

The Garment as Collateral

> If you lend money to one of My people who is poor, do not act with him as a harsh creditor, and do not charge him interest. If you take your neighbor's garment as collateral,

---

10. As is commanded: "That shall be your fringe; **see** it and remember all the commandments of God" (Bemidbar 15:39).

11. Yissachar Jacobson, *Bina Bemikra* (Tel Aviv: Sinai Publishing, 1996), 160.

return it to him before the sun sets, because it is his only clothing, the sole covering for his skin. What else does he have in which to sleep? And if he cries out to Me, I will be listening: I am compassionate. (Shemot 22:24–26)

This passage describes a case of someone lending money to a poor person and accepting his only garment as collateral. God says you must return it to him before sunset; if you do not, and he cries out, God will listen to his cry. Why is God so concerned with the garment? Certainly, there are other ways to mistreat a poor person. The answer is that the garment does not ultimately belong to the poor person or to the lender; it came from God. God generously gave clothing to Adam and Ḥava. A lender, too, should be considerate of those who need clothing. Anyone who ignores that reality will pay a price from God.

Removing a Father's Garment

A man shall not take his father's wife, nor remove the corner [*kanaf*] of his father's [garment]. (Devarim 23:1)

This prohibition sets up a parallel between a son's taking his father's wife and removing the corner of his father's garment. While even the second half of the verse has a sense of sexual impropriety,[12] this entire scenario is also a challenge to the father's authority.[13] By taking away his father's garment (particularly via the *kanaf*, the hem or the corner, whose significance we have seen in the

---

12. See, for example, the story of Noaḥ's nakedness in Bereshit 9:21–23.
13. This is similar to the story of Reuven taking his father's concubine in Bereshit 35:22. In a parallel verse in Devarim 27:20, the connection is even more explicit: "Cursed be he who lies with his father's wife, for he has removed his father's garment."

tzitzit passage), the son is symbolically taking possession of what belongs to his father.[14]

David Cuts Sha'ul's Cloak

> And David got up and stealthily cut off the corner of Sha'ul's robe. Later on, though, David's heart ached for having cut Sha'ul's hem. "Lord forbid that I should do such a thing to my master – to the Lord's own anointed!" he said to his men.
>
> [David said,] "O my father, look – look closely at the corner of your robe in my hand; when I cut off the corner of your robe, I did not kill you."
>
> [Sha'ul said,] "I now know that you will surely become king and that the kingdom of Israel will be established through you." (Shmuel I 24:4–6, 11, 20)

This passage from Shmuel I is explained in Milgrom's essay about tzitzit:

> King Saul has pursued David into the Judean hills. Saul enters a cave and removes his cloak to relieve himself, unaware that David and his men are hiding in the cave. David sneaks up on the unsuspecting Saul and cuts off the hem from his cloak. The text then relates that "afterward, David reproached himself for cutting off part of the hem of Saul's cloak." He said to his men, "The Lord forbid that I should do such a thing." When Saul realizes what David has done, he responds: "I know now that you will become king" (I Sam. 24:6, 20). What was the reason for David's remorse

---

14. In Rut 3:9 and Yeḥezkel 16:8, we find the opposite of removal of the *kanaf* of the garment. In those verses, we find "spreading of the *kanaf*" as a symbol of the union of marriage, where people are connected.

and for Saul's response? The answer rests in the meaning of the hem: It was an extension of Saul's person and authority. David felt remorse for taking it because God had not so ordered. Saul, however, regarded it as a sign from God that his authority had been transferred to David; he was now cut off from the throne.[15]

We previously explored how the mention of "tearing" of the kingdom in the passage discussing God's punishment of Shlomo was reminiscent of the earlier punishment of Sha'ul – which used similar language but comprised the literal tearing of a garment. In this story with Sha'ul and David, we see again how garments and authority are tightly linked.

The connection between David's cutting off the corner of Sha'ul's garment and the earlier story of Sha'ul and Shmuel[16] is reflected in a midrash (*Shoḥar Tov* 57:3) which says Sha'ul knew that David was king because Shmuel's prophecy had been fulfilled.[17]

In all three of these stories concerning the kings,[18] having a garment with corners cut off – i.e., an unfinished garment – indicates they no longer have full authority. The commandment of tzitzit is therefore a daily reminder that we, too, do not have full authority, but rather need to submit to the will of God.

We can now better understand why tearing clothes is a sign of mourning in the Torah. It is not simply an emotional reaction: cutting skin or tearing out hair is forbidden,[19] and we do not find encouragement for other destructive practices, such as breaking dishes. But when clothes are torn, it is a sign that things are so bad

---

15. Jacob Milgrom, *The JPS Torah Commentary: Numbers* (Philadelphia: The Jewish Publication Society, 1990), 410.
16. See Shmuel I 24:4 and Kiel, *Daat Mikra: Shmuel*, ad loc.
17. Kiel, ibid., note 24.
18. In addition to the story of Ahiya and Yorovam mentioned earlier. See above, note 1.
19. Vayikra 19:28; Devarim 14:1.

that we completely concede control to God. When Yehoshua and Kalev tore their clothes, they were asking God to intervene and take control of a situation which otherwise appeared to be lost.

But this is not an everyday occurrence. As Kohelet (3:7) teaches, "There is a time to tear and a time to sew." And the proper understanding of garments – via tzitzit – can help us fulfill his final instruction (12:13): "Fear God and keep His commandments."

WHY DO HUMANS NEED CLOTHES?

We have discussed how clothing should be viewed as a gift from God. However, this leads to a more fundamental question: Why did God create man in such a way that wearing clothes is appropriate? Why did the awareness of nakedness lead to shame? Animals do not have that shame, so why should humans?

Rabbi Samson Raphael Hirsch, in his commentary on the Torah,[20] offers answers to these questions, and in the process explains the commandment of tzitzit as well. He writes that man was created as different from the animals. Animals follow only their hearts and eyes, and are not concerned with God's commands. When Adam was not acting like an animal, he had no reason to be ashamed of his nakedness. His physical body was fulfilling the will of God. But when he ate from the tree and disobeyed the word of God by following his eyes and desires, he began to act like an animal.[21] A "gift of kindness" from God then awoke inside him – the feeling of shame.[22] The internal voice of shame, implanted by God in man, reminds man that he is not an animal and should not act like one – and therefore he should wear clothes. Shame is God's

---

20. Bereshit 2:25, 3:7, 3:21; Bemidbar 15:41.
21. Kohelet also complains about people behaving as animals: "I said in my heart concerning men that God has chosen them, but I have seen that they themselves are as beasts" (Kohelet 3:18).
22. This is reflected in God's rhetorical question to Adam, "Who told you that you were naked?" (Bereshit 3:11). The answer is the awakened emotion of shame.

fallback plan when man does not listen to heteronomous obligations – i.e., divine commandments. God confirmed the importance of shame by giving man clothes after the expulsion from the Garden. Those clothes remind man that he has a higher destiny than the animals and thus needs to listen to the higher authority of God. Clothing tells man that he is human, and that he controls his body (not the other way around).

Rabbi Hirsch also notes that tzitzit remind us of the same thing: to refrain from acting like animals and to listen to the commandments of God.

WHY THE TEST?

This distinction between humans and animals can help us understand a fundamental question about the entire Garden story. Why did God place a forbidden tree in the Garden in the first place? Wasn't this a form of entrapment, a setup leading to the inevitable transgression by Adam and Hava? Therein lies the difference between animals and humans.

Granted, in some ways, they are remarkably similar. As Kohelet states, "The preeminence of man over beast is nothing" (3:19). All animals (including humans) follow their desires – their hearts and eyes – and instinctively focus on short-term benefits. But only humans also have the advanced brain capacity to defer immediate satisfaction in order to achieve long-term goals.[23] God wanted

---

23. Unlike other animals, humans have well-developed prefrontal lobes, which is where the brain solves long-term problems and controls impulsive behavior. A famous modern representation of the tension between these two competing mental processes is the "Marshmallow Test," where a child was offered a choice between one marshmallow immediately or two marshmallows if they waited for a short time. The study was conducted by Walter Mischel, and he found that the children who chose the deferred but greater reward tended to have more successful and healthier lives. Mischel was inspired by the story of temptation in the Garden and notes in his book that he "wondered whether Adam and Eve might have held on to paradise longer if they had plans at the ready to help them resist snakes and apple temptations" (Walter

Adam and Ḥava to think rationally about the future, not just to react; God wanted them to be human. That required the opportunity to pass up the short-term benefit of eating the forbidden in order to remain in God's special place. They needed the ability to make that choice.

While Adam and Ḥava failed that test in the Garden,[24] their descendants are faced with this same challenge daily. This is one of the lessons of Kohelet – not to focus on the futility of our daily toil, but to recognize that the benefits of long-term allegiance to God will pay off.

In Kohelet, Shlomo also complains about a similar test. As we discussed earlier, he writes: "I gave my heart to seek and to search out with wisdom all that happens under the heavens: an evil task that God gave men to be afflicted [*la'anot*] with"[25] (Kohelet 1:13). As seen throughout Kohelet, Shlomo's search for wisdom became a source of his affliction. But why does he blame God for that?

If we look back at Shlomo's initial request from God for wisdom, we find he got more than he asked for. Shlomo asked only for the ability to discern between good and bad, in order to properly judge his people (Melakhim I 3:9), but God granted him much greater wisdom: knowledge of everything in the world (3:12).[26] It was this additional endowment of knowledge that proved so problematic for Shlomo, and in the end was integral to his downfall.

Why, then, did God give him what he never asked for?

I suggest that like the Garden's forbidden Tree of Knowledge, this too was a test.[27] Linguistic support for this argument can be

---

Mischel, *The Marshmallow Test: Mastering Self-Control* [New York: Little, Brown and Company, 2014] 62).

24. Ironically, they tried to be like God, but actually behaved more like animals.

25. Regarding this translation of *la'anot*, see chapter 11, note 2.

26. Kiel, *Daat Mikra: Melakhim*, Melakhim I 3:12.

27. Another affliction is mentioned later in Kohelet (3:10–11):

> I have seen the occupation that God gave mortal man to be afflicted [*la'anot*] with. He made everything right in its proper time; He placed eternity [*ha'olam*]

found in Kohelet's use of *la'anot*, "to afflict." That same verb is found in Devarim, in a discussion of Israel's time in the desert and the manna they ate there:

> Remember that the Lord your God has led you through all this journey of forty years in the wilderness, to afflict you [*anotekha*] by testing you, and to know what was in your heart: to know whether you would keep His commandments or whether you would fail to. He afflicted you [*vaye'ankha*] by leaving you hungry, then feeding you manna...to teach you that one does not live by bread alone, but by all that comes forth from the mouth of the Lord. (Devarim 8:2–3)
>
> In the wilderness He fed you manna ... in order to afflict you [*anotekha*] and to test you, so that in the end it would be well for you. (8:16)

In these verses, we see a connection between affliction and testing. Just as with the tree in the Garden, the manna was a case of

---

in their minds; yet no one ever fathoms what it is that God is forming from beginning to end.

Here, the affliction is not about knowledge but about "eternity": man's desire to live forever (or even to know when death will come). The word for eternity, *ha'olam*, is found in a similar context in the Garden story:

> The Lord God then said, "Now that man has become like one of us, knowing good and bad, he must not be allowed to reach out his hand and take also from the Tree of Life, eat, and live forever [*le'olam*]" (Bereshit 3:22).

Kohelet – and Adam – would love to be able to eat from the Tree of Life, but it is permanently out of reach. While they can never live forever in a divine fashion, they can achieve long life and legacy. The path to achieve this is like the other tests we have seen. They need to use their human faculties and focus on the long term instead of acting like animals, only concerned about the here and now. As Krüger points out (*Qoheleth: A Commentary*, 88), the next verse in Kohelet (3:12) limits people to doing what is good in *their lifetimes* (*velaasot tov behayav*), but "access to the 'tree of (eternal) life' is and remains barred for human beings, according to the will of God."

God providing food with limitations,[28] which was intended as a test of the recipient. The purpose of the test is recorded explicitly in the verses:

- To know what was in their hearts
- To see whether they would keep the commandments or not
- To teach them that man[29] does not live by food alone, but by listening to God
- To benefit them in the end

These tests are indeed difficult and can be perceived as affliction. But they ultimately teach the recipient the lessons necessary for a successful life.[30]

Adam failed his test, and he suffered for the rest of his life. Shlomo, too, was tested by God when he received that extra portion of wisdom. Beyond being a judge, who is tasked with determining the facts of a case, he began determining on his own what was good and what was bad. That should have been left to God's discretion. Shlomo failed that test and was afflicted during his life as a result. But at the end of his life, he learned the lesson the test encompassed.

---

28. See Rashi, Shemot 16:4. He mentions the prohibitions against leaving the manna overnight and collecting it on Shabbat.
29. It is significant that Devarim 8:3 twice uses the word *ha'adam* to mean "man," which has echoes of the same word used to describe Adam in the opening chapters of Bereshit.
30. As the book of Devarim states in the same section we cited above: "Know then in your heart that just as a parent disciplines his child, so the Lord your God disciplines you" (Devarim 8:5). God put the children of Israel through these difficult tests in the same way as a loving parent challenges their children.

The Sanctuary

Chapter 17

The Garden and
the Sanctuary

While humans have been excluded from the Garden of Eden ever since Adam and Ḥava were driven out, there is another site, entry to which is permitted under certain circumstances, which has remarkable parallels with the Garden: the *Mishkan*, the Sanctuary that God commanded Israel to construct in the desert.

On the most basic level, both the Garden and the Sanctuary are spaces where God and man meet. If we look at the verses describing Creation and the Garden, and the construction and design of the Sanctuary, we will find frequent parallels that will support the comparison.[1]

---

1. Comparisons between the Creation and the Garden and the Sanctuary can be found in classical sources such as *Midrash HaGadol*, Shemot 35:31; Josephus, *Antiquities of the Jews* 3:7. The parallels I present here are found in Gordon J. Wenham, "Sanctuary Symbolism in the Garden of Eden Story," *World Congress of Jewish Studies* 9:A (1985): 19–25; Lea Mazor, "The Correlation between the Garden of Eden and the Temple." *Shnaton: An Annual for Biblical and Ancient Near Eastern Studies* 13 (2002): 5–42;

Section Six: The Sanctuary

CREATION AND THE SANCTUARY

וַיַּרְא מֹשֶׁה אֶת־כָּל־הַמְּלָאכָה וְהִנֵּה עָשׂוּ אֹתָהּ כַּאֲשֶׁר צִוָּה יְהוָה כֵּן עָשׂוּ וַיְבָרֶךְ אֹתָם מֹשֶׁה: Moshe **saw** that, **behold, all the work had been done** just as the Lord had commanded – and Moshe blessed them. (Shemot 39:43)	**וַיַּרְא** אֱלֹהִים אֶת־כָּל־אֲשֶׁר עָשָׂה **וְהִנֵּה**־טוֹב מְאֹד וַיְהִי־עֶרֶב וַיְהִי־בֹקֶר יוֹם הַשִּׁשִּׁי: Then God **saw all that He had done**, and **behold**, it was very good. There was evening, and there was morning – the sixth day. (Bereshit 1:31)
וַתֵּכֶל כָּל־**עֲבֹדַת** מִשְׁכַּן אֹהֶל מוֹעֵד וַיַּעֲשׂוּ בְּנֵי יִשְׂרָאֵל כְּכֹל אֲשֶׁר צִוָּה יְהוָה אֶת־מֹשֶׁה כֵּן עָשׂוּ: Thus was **finished** all the **work** on the Tabernacle, the Tent of Meeting. The Israelites did everything exactly as the Lord had commanded Moshe. (Shemot 39:32) וַיָּקֶם אֶת־הֶחָצֵר סָבִיב לַמִּשְׁכָּן וְלַמִּזְבֵּחַ וַיִּתֵּן אֶת־מָסַךְ שַׁעַר הֶחָצֵר **וַיְכַל** מֹשֶׁה אֶת־**הַמְּלָאכָה**: Then he set up the courtyard around the Tabernacle and the altar, and hung the curtain for the courtyard gate. And so Moshe **finished** the **work**. (Shemot 40:33)	**וַיְכֻלּוּ** הַשָּׁמַיִם וְהָאָרֶץ וְכָל־צְבָאָם: **וַיְכַל** אֱלֹהִים בַּיּוֹם הַשְּׁבִיעִי **מְלַאכְתּוֹ** אֲשֶׁר עָשָׂה וַיִּשְׁבֹּת בַּיּוֹם הַשְּׁבִיעִי מִכָּל־**מְלַאכְתּוֹ** אֲשֶׁר עָשָׂה: So the heavens and the earth were **finished**, and all their vast array. On the seventh day God **finished** the **work** that He had done, and on the seventh day He rested from all the **work** that He had done. (Bereshit 2:1–2)

Nehama Leibowitz, *Iyunim Ḥadashim beSefer Shemot* (Jerusalem: World Zionist Organization, 1989), 344–52; Yehuda Kiel, *Daat Mikra: Sefer Bereshit* (Jerusalem: Mossad Harav Kook, 1997), Introduction, 109–117; Rabbi David Fohrman, "Angels in the Tabernacle?" https://www.alephbeta.org/playlist/tabernacle-angels-meaning. Many of the parallels appear in multiple sources.

וַיַּרְא מֹשֶׁה אֶת־כָּל־הַמְּלָאכָה וְהִנֵּה עָשׂוּ אֹתָהּ כַּאֲשֶׁר צִוָּה יְהוָה כֵּן עָשׂוּ **וַיְבָרֶךְ** אֹתָם מֹשֶׁה:	**וַיְבָרֶךְ** אֱלֹהִים אֶת־יוֹם הַשְּׁבִיעִי **וַיְקַדֵּשׁ** אֹתוֹ כִּי בוֹ שָׁבַת מִכָּל־ מְלַאכְתּוֹ אֲשֶׁר־בָּרָא אֱלֹהִים לַעֲשׂוֹת.
Moshe saw that, behold, **all the work** had been done just as the Lord had commanded – and Moshe **blessed** them. (Shemot 39:43)	God **blessed** the seventh day and **sanctified** it, because on it He rested from **all His work**, from all that God had created and done. (Bereshit 2:3)
וַיְהִי בְּיוֹם **כַּלּוֹת** מֹשֶׁה לְהָקִים אֶת־ הַמִּשְׁכָּן וַיִּמְשַׁח אֹתוֹ **וַיְקַדֵּשׁ** אֹתוֹ וְאֶת־ כָּל־כֵּלָיו וְאֶת־הַמִּזְבֵּחַ וְאֶת־כָּל־כֵּלָיו וַיִּמְשָׁחֵם **וַיְקַדֵּשׁ** אֹתָם:	
On the day when Moshe **finished** establishing the Tabernacle, he anointed it and **sanctified** it. He anointed and sanctified the altar, too, and all its utensils. (Bemidbar 7:1)	

At the end of their projects, God and Moshe reviewed all that had been done. The work was fully completed, and God and Moshe gave their blessing and sanctified everything. Several words appear in both texts (emphasized in the Hebrew and the English). Throughout the description of Creation and the construction of the Sanctuary, the verb root A-S-H, "to do," appears frequently and consistently (seven times in the Creation story and over two hundred times in the Sanctuary chapters). Another word that appears more frequently in these passages is *melakha*,[2] "work." And

---

2. This word appears in the Torah almost exclusively (with a few curious exceptions) in connection with the Sanctuary and Shabbat (and the festivals), which is the completion of Creation.

although we have not cited it here, the word *vayehi*,[3] "and there was," also appears many times in both passages.

Looking at the number of days mentioned in each narrative, an additional parallel can be found between Creation and the construction of the Sanctuary.[4] After giving instructions for making the vessels for the Sanctuary, God gives the following order to Moshe: "Take care to make them according to that design that is shown to you on the mountain" (Shemot 25:40). When was Moshe shown the design on the mountain? Immediately before the command to build the Sanctuary, we read, "The glory of the Lord rested on Mount Sinai, and the cloud covered it for six days. On the seventh, He called to Moshe from within the cloud" (24:16).

Just as God created the world in six days[5] and rested on the seventh, so too did God make the design for six days, and on the seventh called for Moshe to show him how to construct the Sanctuary and its vessels.

---

3. Along with the word *yehi*, "let there be," from the same root, H-Y-H. Kiel (*Daat Mikra: Bereshit*, 111) explains how this introductory phrase, found in the context of both Creation and Sanctuary, can help explain a puzzling question regarding the last third of the book of Shemot. The Torah spends chapters 25–30 describing God's commands to Moshe regarding how to build the Sanctuary, and chapters 35–40 detailing the execution of the work as commanded. At first glance, this appears to be needless and lengthy repetition. But a comparison with the Creation story in Bereshit 1 provides a parallel. In the Creation narrative, the word *yehi* is used when God first announces what He is about to create. The word *vayehi* is then used to describe what was created. This exact linguistic division between intent and action appears in the Sanctuary chapters as well.

4. Leibowitz, *Iyunim Ḥadashim BeSefer Shemot*, 349–50.

5. Nahum Sarna notes that the "section of the Torah that contains the instructions for the building of the Tabernacle" (Shemot 25:1–31:11) contains "six literary units," which may be "intended to recall the six days of creation." He then adds, "It can surely be no coincidence that the seventh, and concluding, unit deals with the sabbath." See Nahum M. Sarna, *Exploring Exodus: The Heritage of Biblical Israel* (New York: Schocken Press, 1986), 213.

TO WORK IT AND TO KEEP IT

וְשָׁמְרוּ אֶת־מִשְׁמַרְתּוֹ וְאֶת־מִשְׁמֶרֶת כָּל־הָעֵדָה לִפְנֵי אֹהֶל מוֹעֵד **לַעֲבֹד** אֶת־עֲבֹדַת הַמִּשְׁכָּן: **וְשָׁמְרוּ** אֶת־כָּל־כְּלֵי אֹהֶל מוֹעֵד וְאֶת־מִשְׁמֶרֶת בְּנֵי יִשְׂרָאֵל **לַעֲבֹד** אֶת־עֲבֹדַת הַמִּשְׁכָּן:	וַיִּקַּח יְהוָה אֱלֹהִים אֶת־הָאָדָם וַיַּנִּחֵהוּ בְגַן־עֵדֶן **לְעָבְדָהּ** **וּלְשָׁמְרָהּ:**
[The Levites] shall **keep** his charge and that of the whole community at the Tent of Meeting, doing the **work** of the Tabernacle. Theirs shall be the charge of all the utensils of the Tent of Meeting, and they shall **keep**, too, the charge of the Israelites by doing the **work** of the Tabernacle. (Bemidbar 3:7–8)	The Lord God took the man and placed him in the Garden of Eden **to work it and to keep it.** (Bereshit 2:15)

Adam's task in the Garden was to work it and to keep it, and the Levites had the same responsibility in the Sanctuary – to work it and to keep it.

God is also present in both the Garden and the Sanctuary:

וְנָתַתִּי מִשְׁכָּנִי בְּתוֹכְכֶם.... **וְהִתְהַלַּכְתִּי** בְּתוֹכְכֶם.	וַיִּשְׁמְעוּ אֶת־קוֹל יְהוָה אֱלֹהִים **מִתְהַלֵּךְ** בַּגָּן לְרוּחַ הַיּוֹם
I shall set my Sanctuary in your midst…. I shall **walk about** in your midst. (Vayikra 26:11–12)	They heard the sound of the Lord God **walking about** in the garden in the cool of the day (Bereshit 3:8)

Here, both verses use the rare reflexive verb *hit'halekh*, "to walk about."

Lastly, the cherubim are found in both the Garden (Bereshit 3:24) and the Sanctuary (Shemot 25:18–20). Moreover, the cherubim were stationed to guard the entrance to the Garden (located on the east side), and the entrance gate to the Sanctuary was also on the east side (Shemot 27:13–16).

We have seen many parallels between the Garden and the Sanctuary. But this last one is the most challenging. In the Garden, the cherubim prevent entry. They do not serve that function in the Sanctuary.

The cherubim again appear prominently in Shlomo's upgraded version of the Sanctuary, the Temple.[6] The optimism of the chapters of Melakhim describing the construction and dedication of the Temple suggests that the cherubim would be welcoming Shlomo – and his nation – back into God's estate. However, the pessimistic tone of Kohelet indicates the opposite: All Shlomo's efforts were in vain, and he was banished from God's Presence.

Is there a way that an entry into the Sanctuary can lead to a successful return to the Garden? We will discuss this in the next chapter.

---

6. Twenty times in Melakhim I, 6–8.

Chapter 18

Can We Return to Eden?

Rabbi Samson Raphael Hirsch wrote that when man is completely dedicated to the service of God, he has no need for shame of his physical body, since that body is fulfilling God's commands.[1] Much of the Torah seems to be a desire to return to the Garden, or at least to a comparable state. Does this mean that returning to a state of nakedness is also a goal?

NOAḤ PLANTS A VINEYARD

A form of return to Adam's pre-sin state is found in the story of Noaḥ:[2]

> Noaḥ began to be a man of the land, and he planted a vineyard. He drank some of the wine, became drunk, and uncovered himself in his tent. Ham, father of Kenaan, saw his father's nakedness and told his two brothers who were

---

1. See Rabbi Samson Raphael Hirsch on Bereshit 3:7.
2. Grossman, *Creation: The Story of Beginnings*, 320–324.

outside. Shem and Yefet then took a cloak and put it over both their shoulders. They walked backward and covered their father's nakedness, averting their faces so as not to see the nakedness of their father. Noaḥ woke from his wine and realized what his youngest son had done to him. (Bereshit 9:20–24)

After eating from the tree, Adam gained knowledge and began wearing clothes. To undo the consequences of the expulsion from the Garden, Noaḥ reversed what Adam did. He became intoxicated and removed his clothes. Noaḥ was like early Adam: naked, and without the knowledge the tree provided him. However, as Rabbi Hirsch writes, nakedness is accompanied with shame when man acts sinfully. There is no indication that Noaḥ repented from, or achieved atonement for, his improper intoxication.[3] His nakedness – his attempt to return to the Garden – was inappropriate.

THE TRANSGRESSION OF NADAV AND AVIHU

A similar case to Noaḥ[4] is that of Nadav and Avihu, the sons of Aharon. They were killed by God for performing a service in the Sanctuary that He did not command:

Aharon's sons Nadav and Avihu took their fire pans, put fire in them, and placed incense upon it, and they offered unauthorized fire before the Lord: fire He had not commanded. And fire came forth from before the Lord and consumed them. They died before the Lord. (Vayikra 10:1–2)

---

3. Rashi on Bereshit 9:20 follows the midrashic tradition and criticizes Noaḥ for his behavior in this episode. For an investigation of whether the Torah implies criticism of Noaḥ, see Grossman, *Creation: The Story of Beginnings*, 311-317.
4. Eitam, *VeNahar Yotzei me'Eden*, 148.

A midrash[5] offers suggestions about what sins caused this punishment. One suggestion, based on a verse following their deaths, is intoxication: "You and your sons must not drink wine or other intoxicant when you enter the Tent of Meeting, so that you do not die" (Vayikra 10:9). Another proposition mentioned in that midrash is "they were lacking garments," based on the concluding verse of the section describing the various priestly garments: "They must be worn by Aharon and his sons whenever they enter the Tent of Meeting or approach the altar to minister in the Sanctuary so that they do not incur guilt and die" (Shemot 28:43).

This verse echoes what happened to Nadav and Avihu. An association between lacking garments and their punishment is not surprising.[6] Furthermore, this opinion in the midrash returns us to the Garden. The *Tzeror Hamor* commentary[7] notes that Nadav and Avihu's lack of garments was comparable to Adam and Hava's situation, of whom it was also stated, "the two of them were naked" (Bereshit 2:25).[8] By removing their priestly garments, and (or)

---

5. Vayikra Rabba 20:9. A parallel midrash can be found in *Midrash Tanḥuma* (Buber), Aḥarei Mot 7:3.
6. This midrash says the garment they were lacking was the robe. This is difficult to understand, since there is already a verse mentioning the punishment of death for not wearing the robe just a few verses before this one (Shemot 28:35). Rashi (ibid., v. 43), says "they must be worn" applies to every garment mentioned in the previous verses, so the absence of any of them would warrant death. However, Ramban (ibid., v. 35) writes that "incur guilt and die" refers specifically to the previous verse, i.e., verse 42, which legislates the wearing of breeches. Wearing the breeches was explicitly done to "cover their nakedness" (ibid.). If Nadav and Avihu were punished according to Ramban's opinion, then truly their nakedness was exposed. This has much more far-reaching consequences than lacking any other priestly garment, as we shall see.
7. Vayikra 10:1.
8. The Second Temple-period Jewish philosopher Philo goes so far as to say that Nadav and Avihu weren't only without their priestly garments, they were actually naked. He derives this from the verse, "They approached and they carried [the bodies of Nadav and Avihu] out by their tunics to a place outside the camp" (Vayikra 10:5). According to Philo, if Nadav and Avihu had been wearing tunics, those garments would have been burned along with their bodies, and thus the cousins who carried

being intoxicated, Nadav and Avihu were also trying to return to the primordial state of the Garden by reversing Adam's steps.

Like Noah, Nadav and Avihu's attempt to return to the pre-sin state was unsuccessful, primarily because their actions were not commanded by God. The phrase "as God commanded" appears almost forty times in the sections in Shemot and Vayikra describing the Sanctuary. Adam was expelled from the Garden for not following God's command; it is impossible to return there without full obedience to God's instructions.[9]

UNCLOTHED IN THE SANCTUARY?

Yet there is another instance in the Torah where we find an example of a return to the state of Adam in the Garden, with authorized nakedness, and accompanied by a complete erasure of the sin that would naturally lead to shame. This occurs during the Yom Kippur service (Vayikra 16), where the high priest is completely absolved of his sins (and the sins of the nation) from the past year.

Toward the conclusion of the laws of the service, we find this difficult verse: "Then Aharon shall enter the Tent of Meeting, take off the linen vestments he was wearing when he entered the Holy [of Holies], and leave them there" (Vayikra 16:23).

At this point in the service, the high priest enters the Holy of Holies[10] for the last time that day. This is problematic, because it would seem to indicate he is walking naked in the holy Sanctuary, which is forbidden:

---

the bodies out would not have been able to use them to carry the bodies. Therefore, concludes Philo, the phrase "by their tunics" refers to the tunics of those who carried them out. See *Philo, Legum Allegoria* 2.57–58.

9. Eitam, *VeNahar Yotzei me'Eden*, 153.

10. While the verse says Aharon entered the Tent of Meeting, the Sages (Mishna Yoma 7:4) understood that he also entered the Holy of Holies to retrieve the ladle and the fire pan of the incense.

Do not ascend to My altar with steps, for your nakedness
must not be exposed on it. (Shemot 20:23)

Make them linen trousers to cover their nakedness,
reaching from waist to thigh. They must be worn by Aharon
and his sons whenever they enter the Tent of Meeting or
approach the altar to minister in the Sanctuary so that they
do not incur guilt and die. This shall be a law for Aharon
and his descendants for all time. (Ibid. 28:42–43)

One scholar[11] summarizes the difficulty:

Since antiquity, commentators have been puzzled by [Vayi-
kra 16:23].[12] Taken literally, it means that Aaron was to reen-
ter the Tent, disrobe, and leaving his vestments, proceed in
a nude state to the place of bathing, as indicated in verse
24. This procedure is hardly conceivable. The law of Exodus
20:26 expressly forbids exposure of nakedness near the altar.
Exodus 28:42–43 indicates that the priestly vestments were
fashioned in such a manner to avoid possible exposure of
private parts.

The Sages find ways to address this issue through midrashic interpretation.[13] However, if we read the text on its plain, literal level,

---

11. Baruch A. Levine, *The JPS Torah Commentary: Leviticus* (Philadelphia: The Jewish
    Publication Society, 1989), 107. Avraham Stav (*MiBeit LaParokhet*, 2nd ed. [Jerusa-
    lem: Mossad Harav Kook, 2016], 78) says that what attracts the reader's attention
    is the level of detail included in Vayikra 16:23–24, which is disproportionate to the
    relatively simple act.
12. See, for example, Ramban's commentary on the verse: "And this verse really says to
    us, 'Interpret me!' for it is completely impossible that it would command Aharon
    to go to the Tent of Meeting for no reason, only to remove his clothing, be naked in
    God's Sanctuary, and leave [the garments] there to rot."
13. Rashi, following Yoma 32a, says verse 23 should be understood to have taken place
    after verse 25, so Aharon would have entered the Tent of Meeting only after bathing
    outside it. For further discussion, see Ramban on the verse, and an extensive discus-

and note that the high priest performing his service in the Sanctuary on Yom Kippur achieves complete atonement, then in this service we find a full return to Adam's state before the sin. On a day with no sin, there would be no need for the shame that came with that sin, and the nakedness would have been natural and not improper.

---

sion in Rabbi Mordechai Breuer's *Pirkei Moadot* (Jerusalem: Horeb, 1989), 503–51 (also printed in *Pirkei Mikraot* [Alon Shvut: Tevunot, 2009] 279–316).

Chapter 19

Yom Kippur – Restoring Eden

W e have shown the Sanctuary to be a clear parallel to the Garden. It is now apparent why on Yom Kippur, when the high priest enters its innermost sanctum, there is a replication of Adam in the Garden before the sin.

As discussed earlier, the text's portrayal of the high priest without clothes recalls Adam's state before he was ashamed of his nakedness. There are other components of the Yom Kippur service that also indicate a restoration to that state. For example, in the beginning of the chapter, we find the following:

> After the deaths of Aharon's two sons - when they came close to the Lord and died – the Lord spoke to Moshe. "Tell your brother Aharon," said the Lord to Moshe, "that he may not come at any time into the Holy [of Holies]

inside the inner curtain in front of the cover on the Ark, so that he will not die – for in a cloud above the cover I appear. (Vayikra 16:1–2)

Verse 1 connects the laws of the Yom Kippur service to the story of Nadav and Avihu,[1] who died because they acted improperly in the Sanctuary. In the next verse, the phrase "so that he will not die" is a warning, and should be understood within the context of Nadav and Avihu's death. But it can also be viewed as part of the return to the Garden. Only after the sin was Adam's ultimate death confirmed. If, on Yom Kippur, Aharon returns to a pre-sin state, he will be like Adam before the sin, who "will not die."

Later in the Yom Kippur service comes the taking of the two goats, and letting God decide (by lottery) which should be sacrificed.[2] This is a rectification of the sin of eating from the Tree of Knowledge of good and bad. Normally, if there are two animals where one will be sacrificed and the other not, the human making the sacrifice will determine which is "good" and which is "bad."[3] But by leaving the decision to God, we acknowledge that He is the ultimate source of our values and morality.

Continuing with the service, one of the two goats is sent off to the desert: "But the goat on which the lot fell for Azazel shall be presented alive before the Lord; atonement shall be made over it; it shall be **sent forth** [*leshalaḥ*], away into the wilderness to Azazel" (Vayikra 16:10).

---

1. As Rashi comments on this verse, these instructions are intended to provide a way for Aharon (and all future high priests) to enter the Sanctuary and avoid the punishment of death that befell his sons.
2. See Seforno, Vayikra 16:8.
3. For example, see the law regarding replacing an animal brought as a sacrifice: "One may not exchange it or offer a substitute for it, either **good for bad, or bad for good**" (Vayikra 27:10).

This "sending out" recalls the expulsion of Adam from the Garden:[4] "So the Lord God sent him away [*vayeshalḥeihu*] from the Garden of Eden to work the land from which he had been taken" (Bereshit 3:23).

In the Garden story, Adam the sinner was expelled from the Garden, but on Yom Kippur, the sin-bearing goat is sent away, and man is allowed to stay in God's home. And why is he allowed to stay? Because he takes responsibility for his actions. As Kohelet states: "For there is not a righteous man on earth who does good and doesn't sin" (7:20).

Human beings are imperfect and are destined to fail at times. Nevertheless, to allow the prevention of the same mistakes in the future, God requires that they acknowledge what they have done in the past. Avoiding responsibility was the greater failure of Adam and Ḥava in the Garden:

> They heard the sound of the Lord God walking about in the Garden in the cool of the day, and the man and his wife hid from the Lord God among the trees of the Garden. The Lord God called to the man: "Where are you?" He answered, "I heard Your voice in the Garden, and I was afraid, because I was naked. So I hid." "Who told you," God asked, "that you were naked? Have you eaten from the tree from which I commanded you not to eat?" The man said, "The woman that You gave to be with me – she gave me from the tree, and I ate." Then the Lord God said to the woman, "What is this you have done?" The woman said, "The snake beguiled me, and I ate." (Bereshit 3:8–13)

Repeatedly, Adam and Ḥava refrain from admitting to God what they have done, first by hiding among the trees, then blaming

---

4. Eitam, *VeNahar Yotzei Me'Eden*, 130.

others for their actions. Without an admission of sin, there is no opportunity for repentance and improvement.

To rectify this situation, in the Yom Kippur service, the high priest is commanded to confess the sins of the children of Israel, and as their representative, accept responsibility for them:

> Aharon shall lay both his hands on the head of the live goat and confess over it all the Israelites' iniquities and rebellions, all of their sins, putting them on the head of the goat and then sending it away into the wilderness with the person designated for the task. (Vayikra 16:21)

That confession, *vidui* in Hebrew, is an essential part of the service, and is what turns a complicated ritual into an effective means of reconciliation with God.

On Yom Kippur, the high priest achieves a return to the Garden of Eden. The entrance to the Garden is usually blocked by the cherubim. But on that day, the cherubim of the Sanctuary welcome him in.

While only the high priest enters the Holy of Holies, each person individually takes part in one aspect of the return to Eden on Yom Kippur. Everyone in the nation is obligated to fast.[5] God's only commandment to Adam was to abstain from eating.[6] Therefore, our fasting on Yom Kippur is equivalent to a complete abandonment of Adam's sin and allows for its rectification. By abstaining from eating food, we recreate the moments in the Garden before the fruit was illicitly taken from the Tree of Knowledge.

On a national level, Yom Kippur provides a return to the Garden once every fifty years:

---

5. Vayikra 16:29, 31; 23:27, 29, 32.
6. Eitam, *VeNahar Yotzei me'Eden*, 198.

Then you shall sound the ram's horn. On the tenth day of the seventh month, on the Day of Atonement, you shall sound the horn all across your land. You shall consecrate the fiftieth year and proclaim liberty throughout the land to all its inhabitants. This shall be your Jubilee; each person shall return to his hereditary home, each to his family. The fiftieth year shall be a Jubilee for you. Do not sow, or reap what grows of itself, or harvest the unpruned vines, for it is a Jubilee; it shall be holy to you. You shall eat only directly from the field. (Vayikra 25:9–12)

On Yom Kippur of the Jubilee year, anyone who had been displaced from his original land merits to return. How is that year observed? By abstaining from harvesting and respecting the restrictions on the produce of that land.

Chapter 20

Yom Kippur – An End to Concealment

L et us return to our discussion of the final entrance of the high priest to the Holy of Holies during the Yom Kippur service.

As we read in the previous chapter, Aharon should "not come at any time into the Holy [of Holies] behind the curtain, inside the inner curtain in front of the cover on the Ark ... since [God appears] in a cloud over the cover" (Vayikra 16:2). Rashi[1] explains this verse as follows: "He shall not come into the Holy of Holies except with a **cloud of incense** on the Day of Atonement."

Later in the same chapter, we find a similar description of the incense: "The **cloud from the incense** will screen the cover on

---

1. Quoting Yoma 53a. Rashi presents this as the opinion of the Sages, as opposed to the plain understanding in which God says, "I constantly show Myself there with My pillar of cloud." But see Ibn Ezra and Rashbam, who see the Sages' opinion as the plain understanding of the verse.

top of the [Ark of the] Testimony" (Vayikra 16:13). The incense provided a covering screen, concealing God's full revelation.[2]

My teacher Shimon Heksher provides us with a fascinating insight, a mirror to the nakedness we discussed earlier. Exploring the overall purpose of the incense in the Sanctuary rites, he comments[3] that the cloud of incense served as a screen covering the place where God revealed Himself. In his discussion of the high priest's unusual entrance to the Holy of Holies[4] (Vayikra 16:23), Heksher notes that the previous times Aharon entered the Holy of Holies, he was required to burn the incense. But in this last entrance, the cloud of smoke was no longer present, and he had no obligation to light the incense again. According to the simple reading of the text, Aharon entered not to perform a particular task,[5] but just to stand in the presence of God without the concealing screen of the cloud.[6] Heksher further explains that the entire

---

2. Stav, *MiBeit LaParokhet*, 199, notes that according to Yoma 21b, one of the differences between the First and Second Temples was that in the first, God's Presence was manifest, but in the second, it was absent. Therefore, the purpose of the incense was different in each Temple. In the first (as well as in the Sanctuary before the Temple was built), the incense was intended to conceal God's Presence. In the second, the purpose was to attempt to cause God's Presence to be revealed anew.

3. Heksher, *Va'Ani Lo Bati Ela*, 188.

4. Ibid., 258–59.

5. We learned earlier that entering the Sanctuary without a reason is punishable by death, and if a high priest who is permitted to enter does so without his ritual garments he is also punished with death. But fascinatingly, according to some authorities (Ramban, commentary on *Sefer HaMitzvot*, negative commandment 73; Rabbi Samson Raphael Hirsch on Shemot 28:43), if a priest enters the Sanctuary for no reason and is *also* lacking the requisite garments, he is not punished with death. This unusual situation might be alluding to the scenario mentioned here. The priest has entered the Sanctuary both lacking his clothes and without a particular reason, and instead of death, he achieves a unique intimacy with God.

6. As we saw above (chapter 18, note 12), Ramban writes that "it is completely impossible that [the Torah] would command Aharon to go to the Tent of Meeting for no reason." His comment makes it clear that he would not endorse my interpretation that the high priest did indeed enter the Sanctuary for no reason. However, I think it is possible that his earlier ruling that the high priest does not deserve punishment

preceding service was just to lead up to this moment, because now that atonement had been achieved, the high priest could stand in God's Presence without any barriers or screens. In the language of the Sages, this is "love not dependent on any consideration" (Avot 5:16), since the high priest was no longer trying to achieve anything (in contrast to the earlier part of the service, the goal of which was atonement).

In a way, just as the high priest returned to the state of Adam in the Garden, where he did not need to feel ashamed without any clothes, God, too, at that moment, was, so to speak, without anything covering His Presence.[7]

CLOTHING AND CONCEALMENT

The words for clothing in Hebrew often indicate deception:[8]

בַּד – *bad* – "linen"	בָּדָה – B-D-H – "to fabricate"
מְעִיל – *me'il* – "coat"	מָעַל – M-A-L – "to act unfaithfully"
בֶּגֶד – *beged* – "garment"	בָּגַד – B-G-D – "to betray"

Clothing appears frequently as an element of deception, or concealment of the truth, in Torah narratives:

---

if he enters the Sanctuary lacking both a reason and garments can form the basis for this alternate understanding of the nature of the Yom Kippur service. As we saw earlier with Ibn Ezra's two explanations of tzitzit (chapter 16, note 6), even an explanation that fits the plain meaning of the text but was ultimately dismissed because Jewish law does not follow that approach can enrich our understanding.

7. Perhaps this intimate encounter echoes the description of the cherubim of the Sanctuary, who are present at that moment. According to Yoma 54a–54b, the cherubim were naked, and clinging to one another in a loving embrace.

8. Consider also *ḥalifa*, "suit (or change) of clothes," which derives from the root H-L-F, "to change." The verb has a connotation of deception, as in Bereshit 31:7, where Yaakov accuses his father-in-law, Lavan, of cheating him by "changing [his] wages."

- Adam and Ḥava in the Garden covered up their sin against God with fig leaves (Bereshit 3).
- After Noaḥ became drunk and exposed, his sons needed to cover him up (Bereshit 9).
- Yaakov tricked his father Yitzḥak by dressing up as his twin brother Esav (Bereshit 27).
- Yaakov's sons tricked him by pretending that Yosef's bloody coat was evidence that Yosef had been killed by an animal (Bereshit 37).
- Tamar tricked Yehuda, her father-in-law, by dressing up as a harlot (Bereshit 38).
- The wife of Potifar falsely accused Yosef of assaulting her, using his garment as evidence (Bereshit 39).
- Yosef hid his identity from his brothers by dressing as an Egyptian (Bereshit 41–42).[9]

At its most basic level, clothing covers us up, fabric allows us to fabricate; it doesn't show others who we really are. The concealment clothing provides is usually necessary, since in our world we cannot expose ourselves entirely.[10] But a return to the Garden is a return to a world where we have nothing to hide, where we have no reason for deception or falsehood. The Yom Kippur service provides a taste of that world.

---

9. Rashbam, Bereshit 42:8.
10. While the Hebrew verb root G-L-H, "to reveal, to uncover," frequently has negative connotations regarding exposing what should be hidden – as in *gilui arayot*, forbidden sexual relationships (lit., "uncovering nakedness"), it can also represent man's highest aspiration: *gilui Shekhina*, "revealing God's Presence."

Chapter 21

Which Is Holier –
Linen or *Kilayim*?

T here is a tension between the plain reading of the text, indicating the high priest was unclothed in the Sanctuary, and the rabbinic tradition, which has him undressing outside the confines of the Sanctuary. However, there is no debate that during his service on Yom Kippur, the high priest wore garments that were different from both what he and what the other priests wore throughout the year.

In general, the priests wore the "golden garments" delineated in Shemot 28. But on Yom Kippur, the high priest wore only the linen garments:

> He shall put on the sacred linen tunic with linen undergarments covering his body. He shall bind the linen sash around himself and wrap a linen turban about his head. These are

sacred vestments; he shall immerse himself in water and only then put them on. (Vayikra 16:4)

The instruction to wear fewer garments is an indication that full attire is either unnecessary or inappropriate,[1] so even without full nakedness, by shedding some garments, the high priest is heading in the direction of the state in the Garden, before clothing was necessary.

The linen garments had no positive purpose in the Yom Kippur service. Theoretically, the high priest did not need to wear any clothing at all during the service, but due to the prohibition against nakedness in the Sanctuary, minimal linen garments were required.[2]

However, beyond the issue of quantity of clothing, we see a significant difference between the type of priestly garments worn on Yom Kippur and those worn during the rest of the year. The priestly garments were all made of both wool and linen.[3] The rest of the nation was forbidden to wear such a mixture, known as *kilayim* or *shaatnez* (Vayikra 19:19; Devarim 22:11).

These garments are called *bigdei kodesh*, "holy garments" (Shemot 28:2). We find a connection between *kodesh* (holy) and *kilayim* in a few locations. In the following verse we see the two words used in conjunction with the related prohibition against growing two distinct species in the same vineyard: "Do not sow your vineyard with different species [*kilayim*], or the whole yield – both the crop you have sown and the yield of the vineyard – will be forfeit [*tikdash*]" (Devarim 22:9).

Another place where we find both concepts is in the commandment of tzitzit. As we will see, there is an element of *shaatnez* in tzitzit, and at the end of the passage, we find the following

---

1. See Abrabanel on Vayikra 16.
2. Stav, *MiBeit LaParokhet*, 67–68.
3. Mishna Kilayim 9:1.

imperative/promise: "and you will be holy to your God" (Bemidbar 15:40).

In Milgrom's essay, he emphasizes the strong connection between tzitzit, *kilayim*, and holiness:

> But what is there about the *tsitsit* that would remind its wearer of holiness? The earliest rabbinic sources, perhaps dating back to biblical days, taught that the *tsitsit* are *sha'atnez*, a mixture of wool and linen.... Now the wearing of *sha'atnez* is forbidden to the Israelite... patently because it would resemble some of the priestly garments made from a blend of linen and wool.... Thus, *sha'atnez* is forbidden because it is a holy mixture, reserved exclusively for priests and forbidden to nonpriests. That *sha'atnez* is forbidden because it is holy can be derived from the injunction: "You shall not sow your vineyard with a second kind of seed, else the crop – from the seed you have sown – and the yield of the vineyard (literally) will become sanctified (*tikdash*)" (Deut. 22:9); that is, it will belong not to you but to the Sanctuary. However, early in the rabbinic period it was taught... that every Israelite should wear *tsitsit* made of *sha'atnez*.... Thus, the *tsitsit*, according to the rabbis, are modeled after a priestly garment that is taboo for the rest of Israel!
>
> The *tsitsit*, then, are an exception to the Torah's general injunction against wearing garments of mixed seed. But, in actuality, inhering in this paradox is its ultimate purpose.... It is a conscious attempt to encourage all Israel to aspire to a degree of holiness comparable to that of the priests.[4]

---

4. Milgrom, *The JPS Torah Commentary: Numbers*, 413.

While the argument that the tzitzit "encourage all Israel to aspire to a degree of holiness comparable to that of the priests" is persuasive, is that indeed the highest level of holiness?

There is one priestly garment that is neither *kilayim* nor called *kodesh*: the linen breeches. Unlike the other garments, which are "for glory and splendor" (Shemot 28:2), the linen breeches were only functional, serving to cover the priest's nakedness.[5]

On Yom Kippur, the high priest did not wear any of the garments with *kilayim*. But on the holiest day of the year, when he enters the Holy of Holies, would it not be logical that he would wear the holiest garments?

One answer can be found in the prophecy of Yeḥezkel. He describes a future Temple, purified of the sins of the past, and includes the following:

> This is how it shall be when they approach the gates of the inner courtyard: They will wear linen garments, and no wool shall be upon them when they serve at the gates of the inner courtyard and within. (Yeḥezkel 44:17)

This prophecy is not only about the high priest on Yom Kippur, but about all the priests throughout the year.[6]

Earlier, we mentioned that the woolen threads dyed in *tekhelet* are a sign of our being servants of God, for in biblical times a slave would walk around with a color indicating his owner.[7] But

---

5. Rashbam, Shemot 28:4.
6. This is the view of Radak and Malbim (as opposed to Rashi, who says the verse is discussing only Yom Kippur).
7. See chapter 16, note 9. Menaḥot 43b compares the tzitzit to the seal of a king. Rashi, s.v. *ḥotam*, comments that they would make a seal for slaves as a sign of slavery, and Tosafot, s.v. *ḥotam shel tit*, expands and says therefore the tzitzit are signs of servitude of God. See also Bekhor Shor and Seforno on Bemidbar 15:39, who both write that the tzitzit may be viewed as if their king had placed a stamp on them confirming the wearer is one of his subjects.

perhaps *kilayim* in general (not just the particular dye *tekhelet*) is a sign that God is our owner. It is God's brand or seal, as it were. As a mix of distinct species, *kilayim* is a miniature form of Creation,[8] something reserved only for God. In fact, in the Talmud, R. Elazar claims that *kilayim* is forbidden to all of humanity (not just to Jews), which, interestingly, he deduces from the prohibition against eating from the Tree of Knowledge.[9] Just as taking the fruit involved crossing a boundary and appropriating something that belongs to God, so too does *kilayim* involve a trespass and the improper taking of something holy that belongs to God.

Although *kilayim* is for the most part forbidden, in both our fields and our garments, the priests wear it (and it is also included in the Sanctuary curtains and draperies) to show that they belong to God. The "glory and splendor" (Shemot 28:2) associated with these garments is that of God, not of the priests themselves.

But on Yom Kippur, when we return to the pre-sin state of the Garden, the high priest does not need to be reminded of God as Master. He does not need the *kilayim*, and it is actually prohibited for him to wear them. They would be an inappropriate reminder of our post-sin relationship with God.

The Midrash[10] picks up on the connection between the year-round garments of the high priest and Adam's situation after the sin, saying Adam served as a high priest, bringing offerings to God, wearing the garments God gave him after his expulsion from the Garden. According to the Midrash, the garments God gave Adam were therefore meant to display "glory and splendor."[11] This contrasts with the original fig leaf garments fashioned by Adam and his wife, which were meant only to cover their nakedness. On Yom Kippur, the high priest removes the more dignified garments that

---

8. See Rabbi Samson Raphael Hirsch, Shemot 23:19.
9. Sanhedrin 56b.
10. *Bemidbar Rabba* 4:8; *Midrash Tanḥuma* (Buber), *Toledot* 12.
11. Stav, *MiBeit LaParokhet*, 68.

remind him of his servitude to God and remains with the minimal garments only, in order for him not to be naked. In the future, when we return to our pre-sin relationship with God, the priests will no longer need to wear wool.

As we have seen before, God's gift of clothing to Adam after his sin is parallel to the commandment of tzitzit given after the sin of the spies. Both come to comfort the fallen, but also act as a reminder of their sinful past. Tzitzit are not a sign of an exalted status, but rather a reminder that we are servants of God. This understanding can also explain the final verse of the tzitzit passage (Bemidbar 15:41):

אֲנִי יהוה אֱלֹהֵיכֶם אֲשֶׁר הוֹצֵאתִי אֶתְכֶם מֵאֶרֶץ מִצְרַיִם לִהְיוֹת לָכֶם
לֵאלֹהִים אֲנִי יהוה אֱלֹהֵיכֶם.

Following Rashi's commentary on this verse, I would translate it as: "I am God, your Master, who took you out of the land of Egypt, to become your Master; I am God your Master." God is reminding Israel (with the tzitzit) that He is their Master, and "acquired" that right when He took them out of Egypt.

LEVELS OF HOLINESS

Just as the priestly garments elevate the level of holiness of the priests, so too do the tzitzit grant holiness to the rest of the nation. But the holiness of the *kilayim* and tzitzit is not the ultimate goal. Keeping the laws associated with them is a reminder of our sinful state, and both the priests and the people should be aspiring to an even loftier goal – a return to the Garden, where we did not need that reminder and did not have that shame.

Kohelet, too, is giving us that same message of holiness, even using the metaphor of garments: "Let your clothes at all times be white; let your head never lack ointment" (9:8). On a metaphoric level, we should always aspire to wear the high priest's white linen

Yom Kippur garments and restore our pre-sin relationship with God.[12]

As we will discuss in the next section, Koraḥ (whose story in the Torah immediately follows the tzitzit passage) did not understand that message. He saw the tzitzit, and boldly claimed that "All the community is holy" (Bemidbar 16:3). He lusted after the priesthood, for he felt the "glory and splendor" was for the priests, not for God. He understood the term holy, *kadosh*, to mean "better," not "dedicated." As we shall discover, Moshe proved him wrong.

---

12. Abrabanel on Vayikra 16:5 connects the reference to white clothing in Kohelet 9:8 to the white garments of the high priest.

Section Seven

Rebellion and Redemption

Chapter 22

Rebellion

WHY DOES SHLOMO ALLUDE TO KAYIN AND HEVEL?

We have now shown the connection between Shlomo and the problematic search for knowledge. Shlomo's own choices and the outcome of those choices reflected those of Adam. We've also seen some of the ways to rectify the results of the poor choices they made – be it through tzitzit, the Yom Kippur service, or the advice given throughout the book of Kohelet – to avoid the rationalizations that lead to disloyalty to God.

But that discussion applies only to half of Kohelet – the part reflecting Adam's life. Why does Shlomo, however, allude to Kayin and Hevel in Kohelet? How does he identify with them?

Just as Adam bemoaned the disputes between his children that eventually led to violence, Shlomo might have foreseen and dreaded the upcoming split of his kingdom,[1] eventual civil war,[2]

---

1. Melakhim I 12:16–20.
2. Melakhim I 15:6; Divrei HaYamim II, 13:2–20.

and disagreement over the way to sacrifice[3] (which was the root of the dispute between Kayin and Hevel as well).

According to our understanding of Kohelet, Adam felt responsible for Hevel's death.[4] Shlomo, too, bore guilt over what happened to his descendants.[5] As we saw earlier, Shlomo was punished for his actions: His kingdom was divided between his son Reḥavam and his challenger Yorovam. But was the division a result of his search for knowledge or the way he ruled?

We also saw earlier a third, parallel story including a problematic search for knowledge – the spies. Just as the dispute of Kayin and Hevel follows Adam's story, and the dispute of Yorovam and Reḥavam follows Shlomo's story, a story of dispute follows this one – that of Koraḥ's rebellion. Does it connect to the story of the spies in the same way as the other stories of dispute are results of the actions of Adam and Shlomo?

	Search for knowledge of good and evil	Downfall	Dispute that followed
Adam	Ate from the Tree of Knowledge of Good and Evil	Expulsion from the Garden	Kayin and Hevel
Spies	Reported on the viability of conquering land	Death of the generation in the desert	Koraḥ against Moshe

---

3. Yorovam established shrines to compete with the Temple in Jerusalem (Melakhim I 12:26–33).
4. See chapter 6.
5. See "Shlomo's Legacy Is Fragmented" in chapter 2.

Shlomo	Decided which divine laws did not apply to him	God rejected him, and his descendants would not rule the entire kingdom	Rehavam (kingdom of Yehuda) and Yorovam (kingdom of Israel)

It appears from these stories that a crisis in the relationship between humans and God leads to a conflict between people as well. Let us examine why.

LINGUISTIC PARALLELS IN THE THREE DISPUTES

An effective way to begin answering the above questions is by looking at the common language found in the three stories.

One key verb root found in all three stories is K-U-M, "to rise up." While not an uncommon word in the Tanakh, it strongly represents the act of rebellion and challenge in these three stories. From the story of Kayin and Hevel:

וַיֹּאמֶר קַיִן אֶל־הֶבֶל אָחִיו וַיְהִי בִּהְיוֹתָם בַּשָּׂדֶה **וַיָּקָם** קַיִן אֶל־הֶבֶל
אָחִיו **וַיַּהַרְגֵהוּ**:

Kayin talked to his brother Hevel, and when they were in the field, Kayin **rose up** [*vayakom*] against his brother Hevel and killed him. (Bereshit 4:8)

From the Korah story:

וַיִּקַּח קֹרַח בֶּן־יִצְהָר בֶּן־קְהָת בֶּן־לֵוִי וְדָתָן וַאֲבִירָם בְּנֵי אֱלִיאָב וְאוֹן
בֶּן־פֶּלֶת בְּנֵי רְאוּבֵן. **וַיָּקֻמוּ** לִפְנֵי מֹשֶׁה וַאֲנָשִׁים מִבְּנֵי־יִשְׂרָאֵל חֲמִשִּׁים
וּמָאתָיִם נְשִׂיאֵי עֵדָה קְרִאֵי מוֹעֵד אַנְשֵׁי־שֵׁם.

Koraḥ, son of Yitzhar, son of Kehat, son of Levi, took himself, along with Datan and Aviram sons of Eliav, and On son of Pelet – descendants of Reuven. They **rose up** [*vayakumu*] against Moshe, together with two hundred and fifty Israelite men, leaders of the community, summoned in the assembly, men of repute. (Bemidbar 16:1–2)

And three times in the story of Shlomo:

וַיָּקֶם יהוה שָׂטָן לִשְׁלֹמֹה אֵת הֲדַד הָאֲדֹמִי מִזֶּרַע הַמֶּלֶךְ הוּא בֶּאֱדוֹם:

The Lord **raised up** [*vayakem*] an adversary for Shlomo: Hadad the Edomite, who was of the royal line of Edom. (Melakhim I 11:14)

וַיָּקֶם אֱלֹהִים לוֹ שָׂטָן אֶת־רְזוֹן בֶּן־אֶלְיָדָע אֲשֶׁר בָּרַח מֵאֵת הֲדַדְעֶזֶר
מֶלֶךְ־צוֹבָה אֲדֹנָיו:

And God **raised up** [*vayakem*] Rezon son of Elyada as [Shlomo's] adversary. He had fled from his lord, King Hadadezer of Tzova. (11:23)

וַיְבַקֵּשׁ שְׁלֹמֹה לְהָמִית אֶת־יָרָבְעָם וַיָּקָם יָרָבְעָם וַיִּבְרַח מִצְרַיִם אֶל־
שִׁישַׁק מֶלֶךְ־מִצְרַיִם וַיְהִי בְמִצְרַיִם עַד־מוֹת שְׁלֹמֹה:

Shlomo sought to put Yorovam to death, but Yorovam **arose** [*vayakom*] and fled to Egypt, to King Shishak of Egypt; and he remained in Egypt until Shlomo's death. (11:40)

The connection between *kam* and rebellion is noted by the author of the commentary *Kli Yakar* (Shemot 1:8). That verse mentions a new king who arose [*vayakom*] over Egypt. *Kli Yakar* notes, "It appears that the term *kima* refers to one who rises against his fellow to harm him, as it says, 'Kayin rose up [*vayakom*] against his brother Hevel and killed him' (Bereshit 4:8)." He then quotes a set of verses in the book of Devarim that uses similar language:

> But if the man encounters the betrothed woman in the field, forces her and lies with her, only the man who did this shall die. You shall do nothing to the girl... Just as one man at times rises up [*yakum*] and murders his fellow man, so too here; he came upon her in the field. The betrothed woman may have cried out for help, but no one was there to rescue her. (Devarim 22:25–27)

In addition to the verb *kam*, another relevant word found in this passage is "field," *sadeh*. In the case of the engaged girl, the fact that she is found in a field (as opposed to the city, as described in the previous verses) indicates that no one would be around to save her. A field is therefore a place for people to be when they don't want their actions, such as a crime or a coup, noticed.

As we saw above, Kayin found Hevel in the field before he killed him. We also find in the Shlomo story that the prophet Aḥiya was in a field when he told Yorovam of the plan to rebel against Shlomo: "Around that time, Yorovam was leaving Jerusalem when Aḥiya the Shilonite, the prophet, met him on the way. He was dressed in a new robe, and the two of them were alone in the field" (Melakhim I 11:29).

TEXTUAL PARALLELS BETWEEN THE STORY OF
KAYIN AND HEVEL AND THE KORAḤ STORY

A comparison of verses from the various stories will reveal further linguistic parallels. First, several key words and phrases repeat themselves in the passages in Bereshit and Bemidbar:

וְאֶל־קַיִן וְאֶל־מִנְחָתוֹ לֹא שָׁעָה וַיִּחַר לְקַיִן מְאֹד וַיִּפְּלוּ פָּנָיו: But upon Kayin and **his offering** He did not look with favor. Kayin became **very angry**, and his face fell. (Bereshit 4:5)	וַיִּחַר לְמֹשֶׁה מְאֹד וַיֹּאמֶר אֶל־יְהֹוָה אַל־תֵּפֶן אֶל־מִנְחָתָם לֹא חֲמוֹר אֶחָד מֵהֶם נָשָׂאתִי וְלֹא הֲרֵעֹתִי אֶת־אַחַד מֵהֶם: Moshe became **very angry** and said to the Lord, "Pay no attention to **their offering**. I have not taken a single donkey from them, nor have I wronged any one of them." (Bemidbar 16:15)
וַיֹּאמֶר יְהֹוָה אֶל־קַיִן לָמָּה חָרָה לָךְ וְלָמָּה נָפְלוּ פָנֶיךָ: The Lord said to Kayin: "Why are you angry; why is your **face fallen**?" (Bereshit 4:6)	וַיִּשְׁמַע מֹשֶׁה וַיִּפֹּל עַל־פָּנָיו: When Moshe heard this, he **fell upon his face**. (Bemidbar 16:4)
הֲלוֹא אִם־תֵּיטִיב שְׂאֵת וְאִם לֹא תֵיטִיב לַפֶּתַח חַטָּאת רֹבֵץ וְאֵלֶיךָ תְּשׁוּקָתוֹ וְאַתָּה תִּמְשָׁל־בּוֹ: If you act well, will you not be uplifted? If you fail to act well, sin is crouching at the **entrance**; it longs to have you, but you must rule over it. (Bereshit 4:7)	וַיֵּעָלוּ מֵעַל מִשְׁכַּן־קֹרַח דָּתָן וַאֲבִירָם מִסָּבִיב וְדָתָן וַאֲבִירָם יָצְאוּ נִצָּבִים פֶּתַח אָהֳלֵיהֶם וּנְשֵׁיהֶם וּבְנֵיהֶם וְטַפָּם: So they moved away from around the dwellings of Koraḥ, Datan, and Aviram. Datan and Aviram came out and stood at the **entrance** of their tents with their wives, children, and infants. (Bemidbar 16:27)

וְעַתָּה אָרוּר אָתָּה מִן־הָאֲדָמָה אֲשֶׁר **פָּצְתָה אֶת־פִּיהָ** לָקַחַת אֶת־דְּמֵי אָחִיךָ מִיָּדֶךָ:	אִם־בְּרִיאָה יִבְרָא יְהוָה **וּפָצְתָה** הָאֲדָמָה אֶת־פִּיהָ וּבָלְעָה אֹתָם וְאֶת־ כָּל־אֲשֶׁר לָהֶם וְיָרְדוּ חַיִּים שְׁאֹלָה וִידַעְתֶּם כִּי נִאֲצוּ הָאֲנָשִׁים הָאֵלֶּה אֶת־יְהוָה:
Now you are cursed, more so than **the ground that has opened its mouth** to receive your brother's blood from your hand. (Bereshit 4:11)	But if the Lord creates something entirely new, so that **the ground opens its mouth** and swallows them and all they have, and they go down alive to Sheol, then you will know that these men have provoked the Lord. (Bemidbar 16:30)
וְהֶבֶל הֵבִיא גַם־הוּא מִבְּכֹרוֹת צֹאנוֹ **וּמֵחֶלְבֵהֶן** וַיִּשַׁע יְהוָה אֶל־הֶבֶל וְאֶל־ מִנְחָתוֹ:	כֹּל **חֵלֶב** יִצְהָר וְכָל־**חֵלֶב** תִּירוֹשׁ וְדָגָן רֵאשִׁיתָם אֲשֶׁר־יִתְּנוּ לַיהוָה לְךָ נְתַתִּים. **בִּכּוּרֵי** כָּל־אֲשֶׁר בְּאַרְצָם אֲשֶׁר־יָבִיאוּ לַיהוָה לְךָ יִהְיֶה כָּל־טָהוֹר בְּבֵיתְךָ יֹאכֲלֶנּוּ:
Hevel too **brought** an offering: the **best** portions from the **firstborn** of his flock. The Lord looked favorably on Hevel and his offering. (Bereshit 4:4)	All the **best** of the oil, wine, and grain, the **best** produce that they give to the Lord, I give to you. The **first fruits** of all that is in their land that they **bring** to the Lord will be yours. Anyone who is pure in your household may eat it. (Bemidbar 18:12–13)

The matching phrases in these two stories provide both parallels and mirrors. For example, Kayin, whose offering was rejected, was angry and his face fell, whereas Moshe, whose offering was ultimately accepted, fell on his face and was angry as well. Both stories have sins or sinners waiting at the entrance, with anticipation to see what will happen next. While each narrative has the unique phrase of the ground opening its mouth, in Bereshit it swallows the blood of the righteous Hevel, and in Bemidbar it swallows up the sinful rebels.

Finally, we see a parallel between the successful offering of the firstborn animals[6] of Hevel and the commandment to bring the first fruits that follows the Koraḥ story.[7]

The common lines that run through all these verses are religious service of God, rebellion, and the accompanying results.

---

6. The mention of firstborns here reflects a theme found throughout the Torah, and particularly in these two stories: firstborns defending their status. Kayin, despite being the firstborn, is not the chosen brother. Koraḥ joins up with people from Reuven, the rejected firstborn of Yaakov, and Koraḥ's own motivations may have been due to advancement of junior members of the tribe of Levi (see Rashi on Bemidbar 16:1).

7. Another interesting parallel can be found between the story of Kayin and Hevel, and a set of commandments in the Torah in Vayikra 17. The laws in this chapter require that slaughtering of all animals for food be done within the framework of sacrifice (as opposed to Devarim 12, where no such requirement exists). After the delineation of the laws, the section outlines the proper forms of sacrifice: how to slaughter animals so they will be pleasing to God (v. 6) and not rejected (v. 7). It goes on to discuss the significance of blood: the law decreeing that when blood is spilled it must be covered with earth, and the statement that the life of all creatures is in their blood. Anyone who violates these commandments will be cut off.

There are strong parallels here to the story of Kayin and Hevel. In the pre-Flood period, eating animals was not yet permitted, but animal sacrifice was acceptable. This dovetails with the laws of Vayikra 17, where sacrifice is the only acceptable form of animal slaughter. In Bereshit, Hevel's sacrifice was pleasing to God (Bereshit 4:4), whereas Kayin's was not (v. 5). Hevel's blood was spilled and was covered up by the earth (vv. 10–11). At the end of the narrative, Kayin was banished (v. 12) – "cut off." The Torah does not explain why Kayin's sacrifice was rejected, but if Bereshit 4 is parallel to Vayikra 17, then perhaps Kayin did not follow the rules of ritual slaughter explained in that chapter.

Also worth noting is that the laws in Vayikra 17 immediately follow those of the Yom Kippur service. As we discussed earlier, the Yom Kippur service has many parallels to Adam in the Garden and can be viewed as a rectification of his sin. Similarly, the laws of sacrifices in Vayikra 17 can be seen as a way to correct the mistakes of Kayin.

PARALLELS BETWEEN KORAḤ,

AND SHLOMO AND HIS CHALLENGERS

We can pick up similar threads when comparing the story of Koraḥ with the later events in the life of Yorovam, Shlomo's challenger:

וַיִּשְׁלַח מֹשֶׁה לִקְרֹא לְדָתָן וְלַאֲבִירָם בְּנֵי אֱלִיאָב וַיֹּאמְרוּ לֹא נַעֲלֶה:	וַיִּשְׁלְחוּ וַיִּקְרְאוּ־לוֹ ויבאו [וַיָּבֹא] יָרָבְעָם וְכָל־קְהַל יִשְׂרָאֵל וַיְדַבְּרוּ אֶל־רְחַבְעָם לֵאמֹר:
After this, Moshe **sent to call** Datan and Aviram, sons of Eliav. But they said, "We will not come up." (Bemidbar 16:12)	They **sent and called him**, and Yorovam came with the whole assembly of Israel, who made the following speech to Reḥavam. (Melakhim I 12:3)
וַיָּקֻמוּ לִפְנֵי מֹשֶׁה וַאֲנָשִׁים מִבְּנֵי־יִשְׂרָאֵל חֲמִשִּׁים וּמָאתָיִם נְשִׂיאֵי עֵדָה קְרִאֵי מוֹעֵד אַנְשֵׁי־שֵׁם:	וַיְהִי כִּשְׁמֹעַ כָּל־יִשְׂרָאֵל כִּי־שָׁב יָרָבְעָם וַיִּשְׁלְחוּ וַיִּקְרְאוּ אֹתוֹ אֶל־הָעֵדָה וַיַּמְלִיכוּ אֹתוֹ עַל־כָּל־יִשְׂרָאֵל לֹא הָיָה אַחֲרֵי בֵית־דָּוִד זוּלָתִי שֵׁבֶט־יְהוּדָה לְבַדּוֹ:
They rose up against Moshe, together with two hundred and fifty Israelite men, leaders of the community, **summoned in the assembly**, men of repute. (Bemidbar 16:2)	When all of Israel heard that Yorovam had returned, they sent and **summoned him to the assembly** and made him king over all Israel. Only the tribe of Yehuda followed the House of David. (Melakhim I 12:20)

וַיִּקָּהֲלוּ עַל־מֹשֶׁה וְעַל־אַהֲרֹן וַיֹּאמְרוּ אֲלֵהֶם רַב־לָכֶם כִּי כָל־הָעֵדָה כֻּלָּם קְדֹשִׁים וּבְתוֹכָם יְהוָה וּמַדּוּעַ תִּתְנַשְּׂאוּ עַל־קְהַל יְהוָה:

They gathered against Moshe and Aharon together, and said to them, "**You have gone too far.** All the community is holy, every one of them, and the Lord is in their midst. Why then do you set yourselves above the Lord's people?" (Bemidbar 16:3)

...וְהָיָה הָאִישׁ אֲשֶׁר־יִבְחַר יְהוָה הוּא הַקָּדוֹשׁ רַב־לָכֶם בְּנֵי לֵוִי:

The man whom the Lord chooses – he is holy. It is you, **sons of Levi**, who **have gone too far!** (Bemidbar 16:7)

וַיַּקְרֵב אֹתְךָ וְאֶת־כָּל־אַחֶיךָ בְנֵי־לֵוִי אִתָּךְ וּבִקַּשְׁתֶּם גַּם־כְּהֻנָּה:

He has brought you, and with you all your fellow **sons of Levi**, to be close to Him, and yet you seek the priesthood also? (Bemidbar 16:10)

וַיִּקְחוּ אִישׁ מַחְתָּתוֹ וַיִּתְּנוּ עֲלֵיהֶם אֵשׁ וַיָּשִׂימוּ עֲלֵיהֶם קְטֹרֶת וַיַּעַמְדוּ פֶּתַח אֹהֶל מוֹעֵד וּמֹשֶׁה וְאַהֲרֹן:

Each took his censer, placed fire in it, put **incense** upon it, and stood at the entrance to the Tent of Meeting, as did Moshe and Aharon. (Bemidbar 16:18)

וַיִּוָּעַץ הַמֶּלֶךְ וַיַּעַשׂ שְׁנֵי עֶגְלֵי זָהָב וַיֹּאמֶר אֲלֵהֶם רַב־לָכֶם מֵעֲלוֹת יְרוּשָׁלַם....וַיַּעַשׂ אֶת־בֵּית בָּמוֹת וַיַּעַשׂ כֹּהֲנִים מִקְצוֹת הָעָם אֲשֶׁר לֹא־הָיוּ מִבְּנֵי לֵוִי.

So the king took counsel and made two calves of gold. "It is **too far for you to go** up to Jerusalem," he said to them.... He made buildings for the high shrines and made priests out of an array of people who were not **sons of Levi**. (Melakhim I 12:28–31)

וְהִנֵּה אִישׁ אֱלֹהִים בָּא מִיהוּדָה בִּדְבַר יְהוָה אֶל־בֵּית־אֵל וְיָרָבְעָם עֹמֵד עַל־הַמִּזְבֵּחַ לְהַקְטִיר:

Just then, a man of God from Yehuda arrived at Beit El at the Lord's command; Yorovam was standing on the altar about **to burn incense**. (Melakhim I 13:1)

In both narratives, the rebels are called to the assembly. Both Koraḥ and Yorovam brought incense. Each claimed the religious establishment had gone "too far," but by appointing priests who weren't even from the tribe of Levi, Yorovam went even further than Koraḥ's demands. Finally, the political and religious components of each rebellion were intertwined to the point that the motivations for the actions are not clear.

THE PATTERN OF REBELLION

What does this pattern mean? What is the connection between the political or personal rebellion and the debate over religious practice? And why do these narratives appear in the Tanakh directly after stories of search for knowledge and subsequent downfall? The following theory can help answer these questions.

After the betrayal of God in the downfall stories, the relationship between Him and humans is shattered. In the wake of that crisis, the latter will try innovative approaches to reconnect with God. This vacuum encourages uncertainty and a difference of opinion within the populace regarding what is the right path. In all three stories, there was a weakness to be repaired by people with different approaches to solving the problem.

Ideally, both sides of the human argument should recognize that they might not be completely right. Can they try to work together with those who disagree with them? As Kohelet teaches:

טוֹבִים הַשְּׁנַיִם מִן־הָאֶחָד אֲשֶׁר יֵשׁ־לָהֶם שָׂכָר טוֹב בַּעֲמָלָם.

Two are better than one, for they have greater benefit from their labor. (Kohelet 4:9)

But when one side is in a preferred position, when they are (or claim to be) chosen by God, it leads to jealousy on the other side. And in the cases we explored above, it led to a rebellion, epitomized by the verb K-U-M: they "rise up" against those with whom they disagree. They claimed, "You are using your form of religion and sacrifice to benefit yourself!" This type of rationalization is not unrelated to the sin of betraying God in the stories of Adam, the spies, and Shlomo, where the protagonists decided on their own what was right and what was wrong. Moreover, the pattern of rebellion fits all three stories.

Kayin was a farmer and Hevel was a shepherd; they worked in, and controlled, different territories. God preferred Hevel's animal sacrifice over Kayin's offering of fruits of the soil. If the reason for God's preference was the type of sacrifice, then Hevel, as a shepherd, would have a clear economic (and even political) advantage over Kayin the farmer.[8] Their dispute was about more than just the sacrifice; it was about their way of life. Kayin challenged Hevel's realm of dominion, as well as the right way to serve God.

The relationship between God and Israel was also seriously harmed immediately following the episode of the spies. The people too felt estranged from God, as evidenced by Bemidbar 14:39–45. There we read that after the decree that the generation would not enter the land, a group of people tried to rectify their previous actions by entering the land on their own. But this time God was not with them, and they were defeated.

Moshe's relationship with God was affected as well. According to the Sages,[9] God did not speak to Moshe during the thirty-eight years following the sin of the spies. In this environment, Korah could claim, "Everyone is holy," challenge the way to serve God, and in the process accuse Moshe of wanting the current form of worship to maintain his own power.

Shlomo's story is more complicated. On the one hand, we understand from God's words to Shlomo that the rebellion is a

---

8. Kayin may have already been frustrated that he, unlike Hevel, was following God's command to work the land.
9. Taanit 30b.

punishment for his idolatry. But on the other hand, Yorovam's argument against Shlomo was that he oppressed the people. Shlomo's wisdom was now viewed as a source of his corruption; he built the buildings and took advantage of the people. By betraying God, Shlomo's very act of building the Temple had become, in the eyes of the people, a way of maintaining power. Yorovam followed Koraḥ's lead, said there was no need for the priests to perform the sacrifices, and set up alternate altars.

We have seen the pattern repeat again and again. Is this evidence of an unavoidable cycle, or is there a way forward that can prevent it? Moshe provides us with an answer.

Chapter 23

Redemption

In the three stories of rebellion we have been examining, each divinely chosen leader was destined to suffer an insurrection against him. Hevel was murdered by Kayin, who challenged his status as the chosen brother. Shlomo was challenged by Yorovam and, after Shlomo's death, Yorovam became the leader of all but two of the tribes of Israel. Moshe was indeed challenged by Korah, but even after Korah's rebellion, Moshe remained the undisputed and beloved leader of the people. Why?

The answer is found in the difference between Moshe and Shlomo.

HOW IS MOSHE DIFFERENT FROM SHLOMO?

In Devarim 17, the king is warned not to amass wealth, wives, and horses, and is also commanded to carry a Torah scroll with him at all times. The reason given is:

[In order that] he will not raise his heart above his brothers,
or stray from the commandment[1] to the right or to the left,
so that he and his descendants will reign long in the midst
of Israel. (Devarim 17:20)

Shlomo violated those three prohibitions, and thus was justifiably
accused of raising his heart above his brothers. He was punished
for turning his heart to other gods, i.e., deviating from the commandments. By letting his heart stray from the welfare of his brothers, he indulged in the excesses that ultimately led to Yorovam's
successful rebellion. That rebellion was a divine punishment for
his association with idol worship, as well as a consequence of his
abuse of power.[2]

Moshe, on the other hand, could testify that he had "not taken
a single donkey" from the people (Bemidbar 16:15). This is why
Korah's rebellion failed. Moshe's leadership was not tainted with
corruption or desire for personal gain, and so any allegations of
impure religious motivations would be disregarded.

WHY DID SHLOMO CALL HIMSELF KOHELET?

In light of the above, we can answer a question that we have not
addressed until now: Why did Shlomo refer to himself as Kohelet?

Many suggestions are found in the Midrash and the commentaries. Based on our discussion so far, I propose the following
explanation:

The king is commanded:

---

1. The word *commandment* appearing here in the singular could be a reference to the
   Garden story, when there was only one commandment. It might also be referencing
   the king's charge to always carry a Torah scroll with him. This king-specific commandment calls to mind the commandment of tzitzit, a constant reminder to listen
   to the voice of God and not only to our internal rationalizations.
2. For further discussion of this point, see Yoram Hazony, *The Philosophy of Hebrew
   Scripture* (New York: Cambridge University Press, 2012), 156–59.

As he presides upon his royal throne, he must **write** a copy of **this Torah** for himself upon a scroll that is in the charge of the **Levitical priests**. It must always be with him and he shall read from it all the days of his life, **so that he may learn to revere the Lord his God, taking care to keep all the words of this Torah** and these laws. (Devarim 17:18–19)

Another commandment traditionally identified[3] as an obligation of the king is *hak'hel*, a national assembly held every seven years, where the king reads from the Torah to the people:

> Then Moshe **wrote** down this Torah and gave it to the **priests, sons of Levi**, who carried the Ark of the Covenant of the Lord, and to all the elders of Israel. Moshe then commanded them: "At the end of every seventh year, the sabbatical year, during the festival of Sukkot, when all Israel comes to appear before the Lord your God at the place that He will choose, you shall read out this Law in the presence of all Israel, for them to hear. Gather [*hak'hel*] the people – men, women, and children, including the strangers living in your towns – so that they may **hear and learn to revere the Lord your God and taking care to keep all the words of this Torah**, and so that their children, who do not know it, may listen and learn to be in awe of the Lord your God, as long as you live in the land that you are crossing the Jordan to possess." (Devarim 31:9–13)

The language of the *hak'hel* shares, strikingly, some elements with the law of the king's dedicated Torah. In the first passage, the king must carry a Torah written by the Levitical priests,[4] and in the

---

3. Sotah 7:8.
4. All priests were from the tribe of Levi, i.e., they were "sons of Levi."

second, Moshe gave a Torah to the priests, "sons of Levi," and said it should be read at the *hak'hel* ceremony. In both laws, the purpose of the book of the Torah is to teach the king and the people to fear God and obey His commandments.[5]

The following message appears earlier in Devarim, where Moshe is addressing the people before they enter the land. Once again, we find similar language, including the word *hak'hel*:

> See: I have taught you decrees and laws as the Lord my God commanded me, for you to keep in the land that you are about to enter and possess. **Take care to keep them,** for this will be your wisdom and understanding in the eyes of the peoples: when they hear all these decrees they will say, "Surely this great nation is a wise and understanding [*hakham venavon*] people!" For what other great nation has God so close to it as the Lord our God is to us whenever we call out to Him? And what other great nation has decrees and laws as just as **all this Torah** that I am setting before you today? But take care and be very vigilant not to forget the things that your eyes have seen, nor to let them depart from your heart, as long as you live. Make known to your children and your children's children, how you once stood before the Lord your God at Ḥorev, when the Lord said to me, "Gather [*hak'hel*] the people for Me, and I will **let them hear My words so that they may learn to revere Me** as long as they live on earth, and teach their children likewise." (Devarim 4:5–10)

These verses teach the purpose of the Torah as a whole. God gave us the Torah to be our "wisdom and understanding," and the

---

5. This is also the message that David, at the end of his life, gave to his son Shlomo (Melachim I 2:3–4).

nations of the world will recognize that. But we need to be careful not to forget what we saw. Our hearts must not turn from the path God commanded.

The section in Devarim 17 enumerating the laws of the king is well known for its connection to Shlomo, since he effectively violated all the prohibitions. The passage in Devarim 4 we quoted above is also full of language associated with Shlomo. For example, the phrase *ḥakham venavon*, "wise and understanding," appears only twice in the entire Tanakh, once here, in Devarim 4:6, and once regarding Shlomo's divine gift: "I now do as you have spoken. I give you a wise and understanding [*ḥakham venavon*] heart; there has never been anyone like you before, nor will anyone like you arise again" (Melakhim I 3:12).

Both verses describe incomparable wisdom. And indeed, Shlomo's wisdom was famous among all the nations: "People from all nations came to hear Shlomo's wisdom on behalf of all the kings of the earth who had heard of his wisdom" (Melakhim I 5:14).[6] This verse emphasizes twice that the nations were interested in Shlomo's wisdom. But in Devarim 4, Moshe emphasizes that the Torah itself is "our wisdom." While the divine source of Shlomo's wisdom was clear when he received it, that message was lost further on in Shlomo's reign. As he later mentions in Kohelet: "I tried all this with my wisdom. I said, 'I shall be wiser' but it was far from me" (Kohelet 7:23). Shlomo had constantly been searching for wisdom, but he should have been looking at the Torah, which is "not far from you" (Devarim 30:11).

Moshe's warning of a "departing heart" (Devarim 4:9) also applies directly to Shlomo. God granted him a "listening heart"

---

6. The terms "all the nations" and "all the kings of the earth" emphasize Shlomo's universal scope and recognition. See Appendix 2: "David's Prayer for Shlomo," to see how David hoped such an encounter between "the nations" and Shlomo would unfold.

(Melakhim I 3:9), but in the end, his heart "departed from him"; it led him astray (11:4).

I propose that this is why the book, and its author, are called "Kohelet." Had Shlomo paid attention to the message of the Torah scroll he was commanded to write, he would not have suffered such a downfall. Now, at the end of his life, he is essentially performing his own extended *hak'hel* ceremony. This was the one last opportunity for Shlomo, as the "wisest of all men" (Melakhim I 5:11), to use his divine gift of wisdom. He composed a book of wisdom so that all could learn from him.

The texts read at the *hak'hel* ceremony are enumerated in a mishna,[7] which calls the entire reading *parashat hamelekh*, "the king's portion." One of the texts included in the ceremony is also called *parashat hamelekh* – the laws of the king in Devarim 17.

The mishna also includes a brief story, which sent chills down my spine. It mentions King Agrippa, who was a descendant of Herod the Great (whose ancestors had converted to Judaism). The mishna recounts:

> King Agrippa stood and received it, and read standing, and the Sages praised him. When he reached "You must not set a foreigner over you" (Devarim 17:15), his eyes ran with tears. They said to him, "Fear not, Agrippa, you are our brother, you are our brother, you are our brother!"

If Agrippa cried because he was concerned his lineage was in question, it is hard to imagine how Shlomo, many hundreds of years earlier, would have reacted once he began to violate the explicit royal prohibitions. Against the background of the Agrippa story, one wonders whether Shlomo read the *parashat hamelekh* passage aloud at all, except, perhaps, at the end of his life, when he

---

7. Sotah 7:8.

looked back at all the promise he had, and how it had all become nothing – *hevel*.

People had gathered before Shlomo many times before. For example: "Then Shlomo assembled [*yakhel*].... All the men of Israel assembled [*vayikahalu*] before King Shlomo" (Melakhim I 8:1–2).[8] The difference is that there is no mention of Shlomo reading from the Torah at any assemblies, and the people viewed the wisdom he shared as his, not God's. However, at his last *hak'hel*, during which he read the wisdom of God – he became Kohelet.

THE REDEMPTION OF KOHELET AND SHLOMO

Identifying Shlomo with Kohelet continues in an interesting direction: the debate about the ultimate legitimacy of each. How is Shlomo viewed as a king, and how is Kohelet viewed as a biblical book?

The Talmud describes a debate regarding whether to allow Kohelet to remain in the biblical canon:

> R. Yehuda son of R. Shmuel bar Sheilat said in the name of Rav: The Sages sought to excise the book of Kohelet [from the biblical canon] because its statements contradict each other. And why did they not excise it? Because its beginning consists of matters of Torah and its end consists of matters of Torah.[9]

A similar debate (also in the name of R. Yehuda and Rav) appears in a different passage about Shlomo himself. Having mentioned

---

8. The Midrash (*Kohelet Rabba* 1:2) says the name Kohelet comes from the *hak'hel* ceremony that took place at the dedication of the Temple (during the festival of Sukkot). However, this runs contrary to the evidence we have seen that Kohelet was composed at the end of Shlomo's life.
9. Shabbat 30b.

previously three kings who have no share in the World to Come, they discuss adding one more:

> R. Yehuda says that Rav says: They sought to enumerate one more [King Shlomo]. The image of the face of his father [King David] came and prostrated itself before them [pleading to omit Shlomo from the list], and they paid it no heed. A fire came from heaven and scorched their benches, and they paid it no heed. A divine voice emerged and said to the members of the Great Assembly: "Do you see a man diligent in his business? He shall stand before kings; he shall not stand before obscure men" (Mishlei 22:29). [See the greatness of Shlomo,] who constructed My House (the Temple) before he constructed his house. Moreover, My House he built [quickly,] in just seven years, and his house he constructed in thirteen years. [Therefore,] "He shall stand before kings; he shall not stand before obscure men" [and it is inappropriate to enumerate him among the wicked]. And they paid it no heed. A divine voice emerged and said: "Shall His recompense be as you will it? For you loathe it, so that you must choose, and not I? Therefore, speak what you know" (Iyov 34:33). [Only God, and not the people, determines who has a share in the World to Come.][10]

Shockingly, the Sages considered including Shlomo on their list of wicked kings excluded from the World to Come. Neither the intervention of King David nor the merit of building the Temple helped.[11] What allowed Shlomo to preserve his heavenly reward was God's knowledge of who he really was. Only God could

---

10. Sanhedrin 104b.
11. In light of what we have explored, this should not come as a surprise, as Shlomo repeatedly diverged from the path of his father, and his building of the Temple was a factor in his ultimate downfall.

recognize that Shlomo fully repented and was therefore not deserving of the extraordinary punishment the Sages were arguing for.

Both Kohelet the book and Kohelet the person were candidates for exclusion. The Sages looked at the overwhelming, problematic evidence, and the potentially dangerous example Shlomo (and his book Kohelet) could serve for future generations, and were not willing to take the risk. But a look at the entirety of both Shlomo's contributions and Kohelet's content gives a different picture. Like Shlomo, the book of Kohelet begins with words of Torah and dedication to God. And in the end, through Kohelet, Shlomo returns to an acknowledgment of the importance of faithfulness to God.[12]

---

12. A related disagreement among the Sages is found in this Talmudic passage: "Did [Shlomo] return [to reign], or did he not return? Rav and Shmuel [disagreed about this]: One says he returned, and one says he did not return. The one who says he did not return [reasons that Shlomo was first] a king and [then] an ordinary [person, and did not return to his reign]; and the one who says he returned [reasons that Shlomo was first] a king and [then] an ordinary [person], and [ultimately returned to be] a king" (Sanhedrin 20b). Maharal, in his *Ḥiddushei Aggadot* commentary on this passage, writes that the Sages are not claiming Shlomo was literally dethroned (there is no mention of that in the Tanakh). Rather, when they say he was not king, it means his kingship did not have divine approval. In this light, the disagreement between Rav and Shmuel is about whether Shlomo ultimately restored his relationship with God.

Chapter 24

A Map to Eden

While the first time you pick up the book of Kohelet it appears difficult and contradictory, it might be one of the most important books in the entire Tanakh.

The Tanakh begins with great promise. We read of the creation of the world, and God's confirmation that everything was good. He then created man in His image, and placed him in His garden, providing for all his needs. But soon after, that relationship was shattered, and Adam needed to leave that special place. From there, humanity continued to disappoint God, as recounted in the stories of the Flood and the Tower of Bavel.

God forged a fresh path by choosing Avraham to start a new nation. The ultimate goal of that choice, and the subsequent exodus from Egypt and giving of the Torah, was the building of the Temple and influencing all of humanity in His ways. As we saw when we compared the stories of Adam and the spies, the entry into the Land of Israel could have been a reentry into the Garden of Eden. Sadly, when the generation that witnessed God's miracles in Egypt and the wilderness firsthand rejected that opportunity, the chance for a restoration was lost.[1] Yet as their children entered the land, the hope remained that in the future, the nation would work together to fulfill the destiny God intended for them. Their leader Moshe, just before his death, provided them a way to return to that utopian state:

> See: I have set before you today life and good, and death and evil. For I charge you on this day to love the Lord your God, walk in His ways, and keep His commandments, decrees, and laws. Then you will survive and thrive, and the Lord your God will bless you in the land you are coming into to possess. But if your heart turns away and you do not listen and are led astray, and bow down to other gods and worship them, then I declare to you today that you will certainly perish; you will not live long in the land that you are crossing the Jordan to enter and possess. I call heaven and earth as witnesses against you today: I have set before you life and death, the blessing and the curse. Choose life – so that you and your children may live, loving the Lord your God, heeding His voice and holding fast to Him, for this is your life and the length of your days, living in the land that the Lord swore to give to your ancestors, to Avraham, Yitzhak, and Yaakov. (Devarim 30:15–20)

The choices Moshe offers them – life and death, good and evil – recall the choices Adam made in the Garden. If they recognize that "good and evil" come from God, and follow His rules, then they are choosing "life." They will have long life – in a sense,

---

1. The Talmud teaches that as a result of the unnecessary crying after the report of the spies, tragedies will beset the Jewish people for generations: God told the people, "You wept in vain; [therefore,] I will establish for you weeping for all generations" (Taanit 29a).

they will be eating from the Tree of Life. The formula is simple: to stay in God's land, listen to God's commandments, love God, and do not betray Him by worshipping other gods. But despite the simplicity, it proved difficult for the people to put aside their base instincts even for long-term benefit. For centuries, as a result of their giving in to the temptation of idolatry, God would not give them the blessings Moshe promised.

This began to change with David and Shlomo. Shlomo provided peace to a newly united country (neither marred by the fighting between the tribes as during the reigns of Sha'ul and David, nor threatened by external enemies), built the Temple, and fulfilled the promises God gave Avraham.² He had the chance to use those accomplishments not only to have Israel follow God, but to have all of humanity learn from Israel's example. His dedication of the Temple could have been the long-awaited return to Eden.

Tragically, Shlomo did not succeed, and when his "heart turned away" and he "did not listen," he missed the opportunity. He made the same mistakes as Adam, as he noted in Kohelet: "One who keeps the commandment will know no harm, and a wise heart knows there is a time of judgment" (Kohelet 8:5).

Adam should have kept the one commandment he was entrusted with. He ate from the Tree of Knowledge of good and bad, but in the end, had a difficult life and only came to know terrible things. In his youth, Shlomo was given a wise heart, and was tasked with executing proper judgment. He should have anticipated that at the proper time, judgment would come for his deeds as well.

---

2. Compare the verse, "On that day the Lord made a covenant with Avram: 'To your descendants I will give this land, from the River of Egypt to the great river Euphrates'" (Bereshit 15:18), with the verse, "Shlomo ruled over all the kingdoms from the River [Euphrates] to the land of the Philistines, up to the border of Egypt" (Melakhim I 5:1).

Shlomo learned, as Adam before him, that life is exceedingly difficult, and the methods we think might help us to rescue ourselves turn out to be futile:

> So do not be too righteous, and do not be excessively wise, for why should you become desolate? Do not be too wicked, and never be a fool, for why should you die before your time? Better to grasp the one [righteousness], never loosening your hand upon the other [wisdom], for a God-fearing man will heed both. (Kohelet 7:16–18)

Neither the righteous like Hevel nor the wise like Shlomo were saved from desolation, and of course being wicked like Kayin or a fool like Reḥavam are not the right choices either. We must "grasp" both righteousness and wisdom, and determine the proper balance between them; but most important of all, we need to fear God, and listen to what He tells us.

Heroically, Shlomo turned his tragedy into something we could all benefit from. We do not know if Adam ever regretted his actions and tried to make amends. In fact, we never read of Adam saying anything after the Garden episode.[3] It appears Shlomo could identify with Adam's life, both the good and the bad. He reproduced what Adam would (or should) have said.

However, even though we said earlier that unlike his father David, "there is no sign of Shlomo repenting,"[4] Kohelet is evidence to the contrary. Unlike Adam, Shlomo does speak. And he uses one long speech – the book of Kohelet – to address the mistakes of his past. He ceases rationalizing his sins and accepts God as his

---

3. Even the naming of his children is accredited to Ḥava, not to Adam (Bereshit 4:1, 25).
4. See end of chapter 1.

Judge. Kohelet became his *vidui* (confession),[5] which as we saw in the Yom Kippur service, is necessary for any authentic repentance.

Shlomo's Temple was eventually destroyed, and ever since, we have tried to find a way to restore that special place where the human and the divine can meet. We long for the messianic age, when another son of David will usher in an era of peace and justice. But that time will come only when we correct the errors that have plagued us for generations. King Shlomo, as Kohelet, teaches us how to fix those mistakes and restore our relationship with God, and provides us with a map to return to the Garden of Eden.

---

5. Shlomo's repentance does not appear in the book of Melakhim. This is likely because he did it as a private person, not as the king. Kohelet reflects those personal thoughts.

Appendices

Appendix 1

Why Is Kohelet
Read on Sukkot?

T here is an ancient custom to read Kohelet on the festival of Sukkot.[1] Many reasons for this custom are given, and I will not attempt to determine the original reason here.[2] However, it is clear to me that the theme of Kohelet (as we have understood it in this book) is well matched to the biblical message of the festival of Sukkot.

One common thread in the stories of both Adam and Shlomo is the descent from great promise and seemingly unlimited potential to disgrace and ruin. A close examination of their stories can lead to the conclusion that their prosperity was actually the cause

---

1. *Sukkot* are temporary dwellings, often translated as "booths," and consequently the festival of Sukkot is often referred to as the Festival of Booths.
2. For an extensive discussion of the subject, see Rabbi Yaakov Medan's essay, "*Keriyat Megillat Kohelet BeḤag HaSukkot*," in Bin-Nun and Medan, *Ani Kohelet*, 171–91.

of their downfall, since "the appetite grows with eating." They became obsessed with acquiring the few things that were forbidden to them.

We might think the dangers of abundance apply only to those like Adam and Shlomo who had the entire world before them. But this passage in Devarim shows us that everyone is at risk:

> Take care not to forget the Lord your God, failing to keep His commandments, laws, and decrees, with which I am charging you this day. Otherwise, when you have eaten and been satisfied, and have built good houses and lived in them, when your herds and flocks have multiplied, and your silver and gold have increased, and all that you own has prospered, your heart will grow haughty [וְרָם לְבָבֶךָ – *veram levavekha*], and you will forget the Lord your God who brought you out of the land of Egypt, the house of slaves, who led you through the vast and terrifying wilderness, an arid wasteland with venomous snakes and scorpions, who brought forth water from flint rock for you, and fed you manna in the wilderness.... You will say to yourselves, "My power, the strength of my own hand, have brought me this great wealth." (Devarim 8:11–17)

These verses remind us of the laws of the king (Devarim 17:14–20). For one, the phrase *veram levavekha*, "your heart will grow haughty (lit., rise)," appears in the Torah only here and in the laws of the king: לְבִלְתִּי רוּם־לְבָבוֹ – *levilti room levavo*, "to not act haughtily (lit., raise his heart) above his brothers" (Devarim 17:20). Additionally, the Hebrew root R-B-H, "increase," appears three times in the excerpt above: "multiplied ... increased ... prospered" (Devarim 8:13). That verb is also written three times in the laws of the king regarding the prohibition against amassing horses, wives, and the same "gold and silver" mentioned explicitly in Devarim 17:16–17.

These parallels teach us that just like the king, even ordinary citizens can forget God and not keep the commandments when things go too well.

The passage in Devarim 8 begins with another sign of prosperity that is not mentioned in Devarim 17: building houses. Regarding the king, there is no prohibition against building houses, and in fact, with one curious exception,[3] we find no mention of anyone building a house[4] in the entire Tanakh until the stories of David and Shlomo. They themselves represent the stability of the kingdom, as symbolized by the stability of a house. The stability of both the monarchy and permanent dwellings involves a level of comfort that can lead to the neglect of God. That is a risk the Torah wishes to mitigate.

David needed to reconcile the priorities of building his house with building a House for God. First, David has a house built for himself: "King Hiram of Tyre sent envoys to David with cedar logs, and carpenters and stonemasons, who built a house for David" (Shmuel II 5:11). Later, he wants to build a House for God, but God is reluctant. Ultimately, God agrees that David's son will do it:

> Once the king had settled in his house, and the Lord had granted him repose from all his surrounding enemies, the king said to the prophet Natan, "Look now – I am dwelling

---

3. The one-verse story within the Yaakov narrative: "And Yaakov journeyed on to Sukkot. There he built himself a house and made shelters [*sukkot*] for his livestock; that is why he named the place Sukkot" (Bereshit 33:17). Considering the name Yaakov gave the place, the focus is the *sukkot* – the cattle stalls; and not the house. One might think a house – a dwelling place for people – would be more important, especially as this is the first mention in the Tanakh of someone building a house. This foreshadows how the festival of Sukkot will give weight to temporary *sukkot* over permanent houses.
4. I am referring to the juxtaposition of the verb B-N-H, "to build," and the noun *bayit*, "house," which comprises the description of the actual building of a house. There are laws in the Torah that refer to building houses, and of course houses (which are built) are mentioned, but that verb noun combination appears only in these stories.

in a house of cedar while the Ark of God is dwelling in a tent." "Go – do whatever you have in mind," Natan said to the king, "for the Lord is with you."

But that same night, the word of the Lord came to Natan. "Go, and say to My servant David: Thus says the Lord: Shall you be the one to build a house for Me, for My abode? For I have not dwelt in a house from the day I brought the Israelites out of Egypt to this day; I have roamed in tent and tabernacle. But wherever I roamed, among all the Israelites, have I ever spoken a word to any of the tribes of Israel whom I charged to shepherd My people Israel, saying, 'Why have you not built Me a house of cedar?'...For when your days are done and you lie with your ancestors, I will raise up your own seed after you – the issue of your own loins – and I will establish his kingdom. He will build a house in My name, and I will firmly establish his royal throne forever. I will be a father to him, and he will be a son to Me; and should he do wrong, I will berate him with the rod of mortals and with human afflictions. But My loyalties shall not move from him, as I removed them from Sha'ul, whom I removed before you. And your house and your kingdom will be ever steadfast before you, and your throne will be secure forever." (Shmuel II 7:1–16)

In these verses, God says He never asked for a permanent House, and was satisfied with a temporary Tabernacle[5] and Tent.[6] But just as the people asked for a monarchy (a "house" of kingship),

---

5. Like a sukka. The English word "tabernacle" applies to both a sukka and the *Mishkan/Ohel Moed* (Sanctuary/Tent of Meeting).
6. The Talmud (Sanhedrin 7a) expands on this idea. It quotes God as saying that when the love between Israel and God is strong, He is satisfied dwelling, as it were, in the limited space of the Tabernacle. But when there is discord between them, even the expansive Temple is not large enough.

if they ask for a House for God, they will get it – along with the
risk of no longer feeling vulnerable, and hence dependent on
God. Therefore, God mentions "your house and your kingdom,"[7]
which provides the double imagery of both the House of God and
the House of David (i.e., the monarchy). Both "houses" came as
requests from the people, not as divine obligations, and so the
people are responsible for maintaining the proper level of reliance
on, and confidence in, both.

Ultimately, it is David's son Shlomo who builds God's House.
Indeed, the next time someone "builds" a "house" after the above
excerpt took place is in the reign of Shlomo. Building occurs repeatedly throughout the chapters describing his kingdom. Moreover,
Shlomo boasts in Kohelet about building houses (2:4).

Returning to Devarim 8, the danger inherent in building and
dwelling in "good houses" – that "you will say to yourselves, 'My
power, the strength of my own hand, have brought me this great
wealth'" – applies to all Israelites, not only to the king. The anti-
dote is to remember that God "brought you out of the land of
Egypt," "led you through the vast and terrifying wilderness," and
"fed you manna in the wilderness." The miracles enumerated in
the Devarim passage were obvious; they could not be ignored.
But God was no less involved in our success once we entered the
Land of Israel, no less responsible when we built our houses and
acquired possessions.

While the lesson is important all year long, it is emphasized
most intensely on Sukkot:

---

7. The Judean kingdom fell prey to numerous tragedies because of a succession of evil
kings of the Davidic dynasty in the time of the First Temple. At that time, the house
of the monarchy was again compared to a sukka: "On that day, I will lift up David's
fallen sukka, repair its breaches, and lift up its ruins, rebuild it as it was in days of
yore" (Amos 9:11). In the future, the Davidic dynasty will be like a house, but in the
time of the prophet Amos, it was unstable, like a sukka.

Tell the Israelites: From the fifteenth day of this seventh month, for seven days shall be the Festival of Sukkot to the Lord.... You shall rejoice before the Lord your God for seven days.... For seven days you shall live in booths. All citizens in Israel must live in booths, so that future generations may know that I had the Israelites live in booths when I brought them out of the land of Egypt; I am the Lord your God. (Vayikra 23:34–43)

You shall keep the Festival of Sukkot for seven days, after you have gathered the produce from your threshing floor and winepress. Rejoice in your festival, you and your sons and daughters; your male and female servants; the Levites; and the migrants, orphans, and widows living in your towns.... For the Lord your God will grant you blessing in all your harvest and in all the work of your hands, and you shall be wholly joyful. (Devarim 16:13–15)

Sukkot takes place at harvest time, when we are most likely to rejoice in the abundance and potentially forget God. We leave our good houses and recreate the Sukkot of the wilderness in order to remember and appreciate God's role in every one of our undertakings.

Maimonides presents this idea in *Guide for the Perplexed*:

These festivals ... inculcate both a truth and a moral lesson .... In the case of Sukkot, the truth consists of the perpetuation of the memory of the miracles of the desert throughout the ages. As for the moral lesson, it comprises man's always remembering the days of travail in the days of prosperity, so that his gratitude to God should become great and so that he should achieve humility and submission. Accordingly ... one must leave the house [during Sukkot] and dwell in tabernacles, as is done by the wretched inhabitants of deserts and wastelands, in order that the fact be commemorated that such was our state in ancient times: "That I made the Israelite people live in booths" (Vayikra 23:43). From this we went over to dwell in richly ornamented houses in the best and most fertile place on earth, thanks to the benefaction of God and His promises to our fathers.[8]

According to Maimonides, we leave our houses on Sukkot to remember our time in the wilderness and appreciate the bounty we received from God in the Land of Israel. If we were to remain secure in our houses during our celebration of the harvest, without that "moral lesson" of gratitude, we would risk forgetting where all our blessings came from.

But gratitude to God is not sufficient in itself to prevent the haughtiness that the Torah warns against. Just as the king is warned against "raising his heart above his brothers," so too is every Israelite commanded to include his brothers in his harvest celebration. The festival includes the commandment: "Rejoice in your festival, you and your sons and daughters; your male and female servants; the Levites; and the migrants, orphans, and widows living in your towns" (Devarim 16:14). By including the less fortunate in the celebration, it becomes clear that the bounty of the harvest does not belong to the landowner alone.

Cultivating dependence on God is the main message of Sukkot. The transition from the established houses to the temporary *sukkot* is a mirror image of the move from the wilderness, where our dependence on God was complete, to the Land of Israel, where we might have mistakenly believed we were no longer dependent on God.

This is the lesson both Adam and Shlomo had to learn. Adam left the Garden, where God provided everything, to a life of toil. But

---

8. Maimonides, *Guide for the Perplexed* III.43.

even in this new life, he needed to understand he was still dependent on God, and therefore had to remain obedient to God's will.

Shlomo, too, lived a life of houses. He built his own house, houses for his wives, and of course, the House of God.[9] Inside those solid structures, he felt his success could never be threatened, and his legacy would be permanent. But he, too, learned just how dependent he was on God.[10] As is quoted in his name in the book of Tehillim: "A song of ascents – of Shlomo. Unless the Lord builds the house, its builders labor in vain. Unless the Lord guards the city, the guard keeps watch in vain" (127:1).[11]

As described by Kohelet, at the end of his life, Shlomo understood that the futility of life can overwhelm a human being when their relationship with God is shattered. In the end, Shlomo's houses were no longer stable. The temporality of life could not be averted by building houses of stone.

Ultimately, there is no difference between a temporary booth in the wilderness and a majestic palace in the capital. To grasp eternity, one must connect with the Eternal. That is the message of Kohelet, and it is also the message of Sukkot.

---

9. Goodman (*HaNe'um HaAharon shel Moshe*, 247) notes that as detailed in Melakhim I, 6 and 7, Shlomo devoted more time to his own house than to that of the Temple (thirteen years versus seven years), and Shlomo's house was significantly larger than the Temple as well.

10. God emphasizes this message in His prophecy to Shlomo:

    If you walk before Me … then I will establish your royal throne …. [But] if you and your sons turn away from Me …. I will cast away from My presence the House I have sanctified for My name …. And as for this House, once so exalted, everyone passing by it shall be appalled and shall hiss. And whoever passes by this once-exalted House will reel and hiss and say, "Why did the Lord do such a thing to this land and this House?" and they will answer, "Because they left the Lord, their God. (Melakhim I 9:4–9)

    The success of the House is dependent on following God's laws.

11. The next verse, "In vain do you rise early and stay up late, you who eat the bread of toil" (Tehillim 127:2), is an apt description of Adam's life, reinforcing the connection between Adam and Shlomo that we've discussed throughout this book.

Appendix 2

David's Prayer for Shlomo

E arlier, we examined how David and Shlomo had different relationships with God. What did David expect of Shlomo when he would eventually take the throne? An interesting answer can be found in a close reading of Tehillim 72:

> 1) For Shlomo. God, grant Your judgment to the king, Your justice to the king's son 2) so that he may judge Your people fairly, Your lowly ones with justice. 3) May the mountains yield peace for the people, the hills righteousness; 4) may he bring justice to the lowly people, save the children of the needy, and crush the oppressor. 5) May they revere You as long as the sun shines, as long as the moon glows, for generations untold. 6) May he be like rain falling on mown grass, like showers watering the earth. 7) In his time, may the righteous bloom; may peace abound until the moon ceases to be. 8) May he rule from sea to sea, from the river to the ends of the earth. 9) Let the desert nomads kneel

before him; let his enemies lick the dust; 10) let kings of Tarshish and the isles pay him tribute, kings of Sheva and Seva offer gifts; 11) let all kings bow down to him, and let all nations serve him, 12) for he brings salvation to the needy who cry out, to the lowly with none to help them. 13) He cares about the poor and the needy and saves the lives of the needy, 14) redeeming them from deceit and violence, for their blood is precious in his sight. 15) Long may he live! May he be granted the gold of Sheva; may they always pray on his behalf, blessing him all day long.

In this chapter, David prays for his son, the new king, to have a successful reign. He focuses on Shlomo having a just reign: "so that he may judge Your people fairly, Your lowly ones with justice" (v. 2); "may he bring justice to the lowly people, save the children of the needy, and crush the oppressor" (v. 4).

He predicts that foreign leaders will come to his son, and particularly notes the monarch of Sheva. This famously came true:

When the Queen of Sheva saw all of Shlomo's wisdom and the house he had built, and the fare of his table and how his subjects were seated and his servants' attendance and attire, and his cupbearers and the burnt offerings he offered up in the House of the Lord, she was left breathless. "What I heard in my land about your deeds and your wisdom was true!" she said to the king. (Melakhim I 10:4–6)

However, this is not as David predicted. David anticipated that the visitors would be impressed with his justice. They would praise him because "he brings salvation to the needy who cry out, to the lowly with none to help them" (v. 12) and "He cares about the poor and the needy" (v. 13).

Yet the visiting queen does not mention being impressed with the justice in Shlomo's kingdom.[1] Rather, she talks about the building projects and his wealth, which were components of the oppression the people later complained about. And she mentions *his* wisdom, not the wisdom given him by God.

Later in the chapter, David prays: וְיִתְבָּרְכוּ בוֹ כָּל־גּוֹיִם, "Let all nations be blessed through him" (v. 17). This strongly recalls God's promise to Avraham:

וְנִבְרְכוּ בְךָ כֹּל מִשְׁפְּחֹת הָאֲדָמָה.

And through you, all the families of the earth will be blessed. (Bereshit 12:3)

Had Shlomo followed David's instruction, Avraham's destiny would have finally been fulfilled at that time. But in the end, David's prayer, like God's gift of wisdom to Shlomo, became a missed opportunity. David's vision was postponed to messianic times, as prophesied by the prophet Yeshayahu:

This will be in days to come: The mountain of the Lord's House will be rooted firm, the highest of mountains, raised high above all hills, and all the nations will stream to it. Many peoples will come, saying: "Come, let us go up to the mount of the Lord, to the House of Yaakov's God; He will teach us of His ways; we will walk in His pathways" – for teaching will come forth from Zion, from Jerusalem, the Lord's word. (Yeshayahu 2:2–3)

---

1. She does tell Shlomo that God "appointed you as king to administer justice and righteousness" (Melakhim I 10:9), but that does not necessarily indicate he was fulfilling his charge. It was rather a confirmation of God's original gift to Shlomo, where his wisdom would be used for that purpose.

References

Bibliography

Anderson, William. H. U. "The Curse of Work in Qoheleth: An Exposé of Genesis 3:17–19 in Ecclesiastes." *EQ* 70.2 (1998): 99–113.

Antic, Radiša. "Cain, Abel, Seth, and the Meaning of Human Life as Portrayed in the Books of Genesis and Ecclesiastes." *Andrews University Seminary Studies* 44.2 (2006): 203–211.

Bin-Nun, Yoel, and Yaakov Medan. *Ani Kohelet*. Jerusalem: Maggid Books, 2017.

Breuer, Mordechai. *Pirkei Mikraot*. Alon Shvut: Tevunot, 2009.

——— . *Pirkei Moadot*. Jerusalem: Horeb, 1989.

Clemens, David M. "The Law of Sin and Death: Ecclesiastes and Genesis 1–3." *Themelios* 19.3 (1994): 5–8.

Dell, Katharine J., and Will Kynes. *Reading Ecclesiastes Intertextually*. London: Bloomsbury Publishing, 2015.

Ehrlich, Avi. *Ancient Zionism: The Biblical Origins of the National Idea*. New York: The Free Press, 1995.

Eitam, Uriel. *VeNahar Yotzeh Me'Eden – Shorsheihem shel Moadei HaShana BeFarashat Gan Eden: Rosh Hashana, Yom Kippur, Sukkot*. Yeruham: Yeshivat HaHesder Yeruham, 2018.

Even-Israel Steinsaltz, Adin. *The Noé Edition Koren Talmud Bavli.* The William Davidson Talmud digital edition. N.d., https://www.sefaria.org/texts/Talmud.

Fohrman, David. "Angels in the Tabernacle?" N.d. https://www.alephbeta.org/playlist/tabernacle-angels-meaning.

————. *The Beast that Crouches at the Door.* Jerusalem: Devora Publishing, 2008.

————. "Eicha and Ayekah: Was There a Tisha B'Av in Eden?" N.d. https://www.alephbeta.org/playlist/megillat-eicha-and-ayekah-in-eden.

Fox, Michael V. *The JPS Bible Commentary: Ecclesiastes.* Philadelphia: The Jewish Publication Society, 2004.

Goodman, Micha. *HaNe'um HaAharon shel Moshe.* Or Yehuda: Kinneret, Zmora-Bitan, Dvir, 2014.

Gordis, Robert. *Koheleth: The Man and His World – A Study of Ecclesiastes.* New York: Schocken Press, 1968.

Grossman, Jonathan. *Creation: The Story of Beginnings.* Jerusalem: Maggid Books, 2019.

Hazony, Yoram. *The Philosophy of Hebrew Scripture.* New York: Cambridge University Press, 2012.

Heksher, Shimon. *Va'Ani Lo Bati Ela.* Ein Tzurim: Mishlabim, 2015.

The Holy Scriptures. Jerusalem: Koren Publishers, 1984.

Jacobson, Yissachar. *Bina Bemikra.* Tel Aviv: Sinai Publishing, 1996.

Kaplan, Aryeh. *The Living Torah.* Brooklyn: Maznaim Publishing Corporation, 1981.

Katzenellenbogen, Mordechai Leib, ed. *Torat Haim: Kohelet–Eikha.* Jerusalem: Mossad Harav Kook, 2012.

Kiel, Yehuda. *Daat Mikra: Bereshit.* Jerusalem: Mossad Harav Kook, 1997.

————. *Daat Mikra: Melakhim.* Jerusalem: Mossad Harav Kook, 1989.

————. *Daat Mikra: Shmuel.* Jerusalem: Mossad Harav Kook, 1981.

Krüger, Thomas. *Qoheleth: A Commentary*. Minneapolis: Fortress Press, 2004.

Leibowitz, Nehama. *Iyunim Ḥadashim beSefer Shemot*. Jerusalem: World Zionist Organization, 1989.

Levine, Baruch A. *The JPS Torah Commentary: Leviticus*. Philadelphia: The Jewish Publication Society, 1989.

Licht, Jacob. *A Commentary on the Book of Numbers*. Vol. 2. Jerusalem: Magnes Press, 1991.

Maimonides, Moses. *The Guide for the Perplexed*. Translated by Shlomo Pines. Chicago: University of Chicago Press, 1963.

Mazor, Lea. "The Correlation between the Garden of Eden and the Temple." *Shnaton: An Annual for Biblical and Ancient Near Eastern Studies* 13 (2002): 5–42.

Meek, Russell L. "The Meaning of Hebel in Qohelet: An Intertextual Suggestion." In *The Words of the Wise Are Like Goads: Engaging Qoheleth in the 21st Century*. Edited by Mark J. Boda, 241–56. Winona Lake, Indiana: Eisenbrauns, 2013.

Meltzer, Feivel. "Rut." In *Daat Mikra: Ḥamesh Megillot*. Jerusalem: Mossad Harav Kook, 1990.

Milgrom, Jacob. *The JPS Torah Commentary: Numbers*. Philadelphia: The Jewish Publication Society, 1990.

Mischel, Walter. *The Marshmallow Test: Mastering Self-Control*. New York: Little, Brown and Company, 2014.

Moxham, Raymond. "Qohelet's Fall: The Use of Genesis 2–4 in the Book of Ecclesiastes." Master's thesis, University of Otago, 2015.

Sarna, Nahum M. *Exploring Exodus: The Heritage of Biblical Israel*. New York: Schocken Press, 1986.

Stav, Avraham. *MiBeit LaParokhet*. 2nd ed. Jerusalem: Mossad Harav Kook, 2016.

Tanakh: The Holy Scriptures. Philadelphia: The Jewish Publication Society, 1985.

The Tanach, Stone Edition. Brooklyn: Mesorah Publications, 1998.

Toews, Brian G. "The Story of Abel: The Narrative Substructure of Ecclesiastes." Paper presented at the ETS meeting, Nov. 2007.

Twersky, Yitzchak. *Amittah shel Torah*. Southfield, MI: Targum Press, 2007.

Uriel, Yoav. *Megillat Kohelet: Klal U'prat*. Jerusalem: Bnei Zion, 2016.

Wenham, Gordon J. "Sanctuary Symbolism in the Garden of Eden Story." *World Congress of Jewish Studies* 9:A (1985): 19–25.

Zer-Kavod, Mordekhai. "Kohelet." In *Daat Mikra: Ḥamesh Megillot*. Jerusalem: Mossad Harav Kook, 1990.

Transliterations of Biblical Names and Texts Mentioned in This Book

Hebrew	English
Adoniya	Adonijah
Aharon	Aaron
Aḥiya	Ahijah
Avihu	Abihu
Aviram	Abiram
Avraham	Abraham
Avram	Abram
Batsheva	Bathsheba

References

Ḥava	Eve
Ḥizkiya	Hezekiah
Datan	Dathan
Efrayim	Ephraim
Eliav	Eliab
Elyada	Eliada
Esav	Esau
Hevel	Abel
Kalev	Caleb
Kayin	Cain
Kehat	Kehath
Kilyon	Chilion
Lemekh	Lamech
Moshe	Moses
Nadav	Nadab
Natan	Nathan
Pelet	Peleth
Potifar	Potiphar
Reḥavam	Rehoboam
Reuven	Reuben
Sha'ul	Saul
Shet	Seth

Shimi	Shimei
Shlomo	Solomon.
Yaakov	Jacob
Yorovam	Jeroboam
Yedidya	Jedidiah
Yefet	Japheth
Yehoshua	Joshua
Yehuda	Judah
Yeshayahu	Isaiah
Yitzḥak	Isaac
Yitzhar	Izhar
Yosef	Joseph
Yoshiyahu	Josiah

TEXTS

Hebrew	English
Bemidbar	Numbers
Bereshit	Genesis
Devarim	Deuteronomy
Divrei HaYamim	Chronicles
Eikha	Lamentations
Esther	Esther

References

Hoshea	Hosea
Iyov	Job
Kohelet	Ecclesiastes
Melakhim	Kings
Mishlei	Proverbs
Rut	Ruth
Shemot	Exodus
Shir HaShirim	Song of Songs
Shmuel	Samuel
Tehillim	Psalms
Vayikra	Leviticus
Yeḥezkel	Ezekiel
Yehoshua	Joshua
Yeshayahu	Isaiah
Yirmeyahu	Jeremiah

Glossary

Hebrew Term	Definition
adam/Adam	man; the name of the first human
cherubim	a type of angel; figures of those angels placed on the cover of the Ark in the Sanctuary
hak'hel	a national assembly held every seven years, where the king reads from the Torah to the people
hevel/Hevel	breath; futility; Adam's second son
kanaf	corner or hem (of a garment)
kilayim	a forbidden mixture of different species
kodesh	holiness/holy
Maapilim	a group from the children of Israel who defied the decree to remain in the wilderness, and tried entering the Land of Israel (see Bemidbar 14:40–45)

megillot	scrolls; the body of work comprising the five scrolls of the Tanakh (Shir HaShirim, Rut, Eikha, Kohelet, Esther)
Midrash/midrash	an ancient body of interpretation of the biblical text; a single paragraph of the work
Mishkan	the portable sanctuary built by Israel in the desert
Mishna/mishna	an ancient collection of Jewish oral law; a single paragraph of the work
mishpat	judgment
pe'a	corners of a field left for the poor
shaatnez	a garment containing both wool and linen, one of the categories of kilayim
sukkot/Sukkot	temporary dwellings, often translated as "booths"; one of the three Jewish pilgrimage festivals, commemorated by sitting in booths
Talmud	the central text of rabbinic Judaism, comprising the Mishna and its commentary (the Gemara)
tekhelet	a blue dye, highly valued in the ancient world
tzitzit	ritual fringes worn on the corners of garments
vidui	confession (of sin)

Index of Biblical Sources

The fonts used in this book are from the Arno family

Maggid Books
The best of contemporary Jewish thought from
Koren Publishers Jerusalem Ltd.